Presented to:

Dorothy, Alex, Andrea

From:

Justine & D. David

Merry Christmas and
Blessings on The New Year

MOMENTS
that Matter

INSPIRATIONAL THOUGHTS FOR EACH DAY OF THE YEAR

CATHERINE MARSHALL

J. COUNTRYMAN
NASHVILLE, TENNESSEE

January

Nothing gives God greater pleasure
than to help His children.

SIMPLE AND PROFOUND

Hold fast the pattern of sound words
which you have heard . . . in faith and love.

2 TIMOTHY 1:13

As a young child, I can remember the warmth and strength of my father's arms as I nestled there, content to sit silently while he carried on leisurely conversations with grown-ups. Just as clearly, I can remember Mother's firm hand on my forehead when I was sick, the deliciousness of ice-cold apple scraped with a silver spoon for a fevered tongue, the stories she read aloud during bouts with the measles or chicken pox. I learned early that stories were experiences, entrancing lands to which the gates were always invitingly open.

It was an awareness of God's love at its simplest and most profound.

UNDERSTANDING AFTER OBEDIENCE

Cause me to know the way in which
I should walk, for I lift up my soul to You.

PSALM 143:8

God told Abraham to uproot himself and his family: "Get out of your country, from your family and from your father's house, to a land that I will show you. I will make you a great nation; I will bless you . . . and you shall be a blessing" (Gen. 12:11–12).

There was a word of command. There was the promise of blessing. There was no option to ask "why?" or "Please explain everything to me." Always and always the understanding comes *after* the obedience.

So Abraham obeyed. "He went out, not knowing where he was going" (Heb. 11:8). He did not need to know because God knew. And the result of this "blind" obedience has blessed uncounted millions down all the generations.

CHRIST IN THE DAILY DECISIONS

The steps of a good man are ordered
by the LORD, and He delights in his way.

PSALM 37:23

When we learn to listen to Christ's voice for the daily decisions we begin to know Him personally. Most people are astonished at His interest in the details of this relationship. How well He knows us, all the little things we thought we had successfully hidden; how realistic and relevant are the directions that He gives us.

Substituting a type of super-spirituality for Jesus' homespun practicality can be one subtle way many of us try to keep a safe distance between Him and us. C. S. Lewis humorously illustrates this by telling us one way we can "render our prayers innocuous": make sure they're always very "spiritual"—be concerned with the state of another's soul, for instance, rather than her rheumatism.

GOD'S SHIELDING PRESENCE

*In everything give thanks; for this
is the will of God in Christ Jesus for you.*

1 THESSALONIANS 5:18

Recently I've been learning that life comes down to this: God is in everything. Regardless of what difficulties I am experiencing at the moment, or what things aren't as I would like them to be, I look at the circumstances and I say, "Lord, what are you trying to teach me in these things? What do You want me to learn about this?" instead of making my first request, "Lord, change this for me."

GOD'S GREAT OUTDOORS

*The earth is the LORD'S, and all its fullness,
the world and those who dwell therein.*

PSALM 24:1

n the Gospels we are told that it was Jesus'
custom to rise before dawn and slip outdoors to
pray. A hillside or lakeside was His favorite spot for
teaching (Matt. 13:1–2). A boat pushed out from the shore made
a perfect pulpit (Mark 4:1). An olive grove in the Garden of
Gethsemane was a favorite spot.

God's handiwork in nature fed and refreshed Christ's spirit
(Mark 6:46–47). . . .

Jaded by noise, jostled by people, harassed by things, we
who live in the twenty[-first] century need to ponder and follow
Jesus' example. We, too, need to slip away to be refreshed in the
quietness and beauty of God's great outdoors.

HEARTS FULL OF JOY

In Your presence is fullness of joy;
at Your right hand are pleasures forevermore.

PSALM 16:11

When Queen Elizabeth II is at home in London, her standard flies over Buckingham Palace as a sign she is in residence. Similarly in prayer, joy is the sign of the King's approval.

It is possible to find the way to pray with joy, even in a very serious and seemingly tragic situation. Do you need healing? Ask yourself why you want health. Make a series of happy pictures in your mind of the creative ways in which you could use health.

Do you need financial help? Ask yourself how you would use adequate material resources. Create a series of joyous pictures in your mind of the ways you would use money. When these mental pictures reach the emotional level, so that you feel joy in thinking of them, and when you know that God can stand over against your sanctified day-dreaming and smile His approval, then you may know that the answer to your prayer is already on the way.

PRESENT-TENSE FAITH

So I tell you, whatever you pray for and ask,
believe you have got it and you shall have it.

MARK 11:24, PHILLIPS

*H*ope must be in the future tense. Faith, to be faith, must always be in the present tense. Hope is the stepping-stone to faith, but only faith will forgive sins or heal. Every time Jesus either forgave sin or healed, He was putting into practice the principle given us in Mark 11:24. Zaccheus had been a lifetime in sin, yet Jesus said, "*This* day has salvation come to thy house" (Luke 19:9). The man at the Pool of Bethsaida had been a cripple for thirty-eight years. Yet Jesus told him to pick up his mat and walk *now* (John 5:8).

We, being finite, see time as with blinders on in three compartments—past, present, and future. God would have us accept time as it is in the kingdom and in reality . . . the timeless, ever-present *now*.

UNMERITED FAVOR

We love Him because He first loved us.

1 JOHN 4:19

When a child behaves badly, the child's mother loves him just the same. She may be grieved, disappointed, hurt to the point of being angry, but nothing the child can do will ever destroy her love. If that is true of imperfect human love, how much more so God's love!

It is God's nature to love us. Nothing we can do or fail to do can stop the shining of that great love. Our misdeeds often make us turn our backs on God's love. In that case, we have left Him—He has not left us. He is still there loving us, yearning over us.

This is what the New Testament means by one of its oft-repeated words "grace." Grace is "the unmerited favor of God." If we doubt it, we have only to look at the Cross.

JOY IN JESUS

Now may the God of hope
fill you with all joy and peace.

ROMANS 15:13

As I have come to treasure many parts of the Gospels, I have marked in my Bible the passages about joy, happiness, and humor. There are an amazing number of them. Indeed Jesus could scarcely say enough about joy.

We are *not* invited to a relationship that will take away our fun but are invited "to enter into the joy of our Lord" (Matt. 25:21). The purpose of His coming to earth and of all His teaching, Jesus said, was in order that our *joy might be full* (John 15:11). We are to ask the Father for everything in Jesus' Name, *and we will receive that our joy may be full*—and on and on (John 16:24).

No wonder the young in the full tide of life adored Christ and left everything to be with Him!

MISSING THE MARK

The LORD shall preserve you from all evil;
He shall preserve your soul.

PSALM 121:7

Sin is in the world. And sin is "missing the mark," missing God's perfect plan. There is so much of this missing the mark that it is going to impinge on every person's life at some points.

If God left us with only this, real happiness or victory in this life would be an impossible mirage. But the gospel truly is good news. The news is that there is no situation—no breakage, no loss, no grief, no sin, no mess—so dreadful that out of it God cannot bring good, total good, not just "spiritual" good, if we will allow Him to.

Our God is the Divine Alchemist. He can take junk from the rubbish heap of life and melting this base refuse in the pure fire of His love, hand us back gold.

OUR SOVEREIGN GOD

They cried out to the LORD in their trouble,
and He saved them out of their distresses.

PSALM 107:19

Like a great bell tolling and tolling over all the land, deep-throated, its echoes ringing in our ears, the consistent voice of the sovereign power of God reverberates throughout Old Testament and New. He is the God of the supernatural—omnipotent, omnipresent, omniscient in this life and the next. We cannot believe this and also think that our God is no match for the evil of the world.

Yet even believing in God's power doesn't help in our crisis situations if we cannot also believe that He wants to help *us*. Frequently, we hear people say, "I know God has power—if it's His will to use it . . ."—like that leper who pleaded with Jesus, "Lord, if You only choose, You can cleanse me."

Jesus' ringing response leaves no doubt: "I *do* choose, be cleansed."

14

EXUBERANT JOY

I will rejoice in the LORD,
I will joy in the God of my salvation.

HABAKKUK 3:18

Paul and Silas were cruelly beaten at Philippi and put in jail under maximum security with their feet chained in stocks (Acts 16:19–40).

In this crisis the prisoners gave themselves to prayer, which is understandable. But to praise? So exuberant did their rejoicing become that it flowed over from words of thanksgiving into songs of praise.

Praise for what? We might ask cynically. That their backs were raw and bleeding from the stripes so cruelly laid upon them! That they were in prison with all the city authorities against them? That with their feet in stocks, they couldn't even move around their cell? Thanking God for that? From any human point of view, it makes no sense. It's foolishness, maybe even hypocrisy. Foolishness, that is, so long as we are looking at the human circumstances and not at God.

HELP WITH EVERY LITTLE THING

But the very hairs of your head are all numbered.
Do not fear therefore; you are of more value than many sparrows.

MATTHEW 10:30–31

God's love for you is so individual, Jesus told us He even has the hairs of your head numbered. Well, since that's true, surely He knows every little thing about each one of us and wants us to ask for His help with every little thing. But He does insist that we *ask*. Having had the courage and audacity to give us free will, God respects that always and forever. He will not crash the door of our hearts. We have to *want* Him in our lives!

Of course, we shall be foolish indeed if we do not want Him. If we are foolish enough to think that we can manage without His help and wisdom in making decisions; His strength and stability when we hit difficulties and rough spots; His gentleness and love and understanding to keep us from getting hard-hearted, rough, and cynical—then we are the losers.

DOES GOD CARE?

Trust in the LORD with all your heart,
and lean not on your own understanding.

PROVERBS 3:5

After the death of my baby granddaughter, I went through a period of rebellion. "Is God really involved? Does He care what happens to us as Christians?" Eventually I had to give up and drop my rebellion. This is what we have to do when we don't understand why God allows certain things. We have the choice of rebelling against God the rest of our days or else being humble enough to lay our rebellion down at the Lord's feet, admitting, "I don't understand, but I want You more than I want my screaming rebellion." Only when we humble ourselves before Him is He going to be able to give us any real understanding.

THE VINE AND THE BRANCHES

Without me, you can do nothing.

JOHN 15:5

*N*othing? That seems a trifle sweeping. Perhaps Jesus meant simply that we shall be more effective with His help than without it.

But when we go back to the context in which the statement is made, we find that Jesus meant precisely what He said. This is the allegory of the vine and the branches: "I am the vine, you are the branches." The point is not that the branches will do better when they are attached to the vine. Unless attached, the branches must wither and die.

GOD'S GUIDANCE

You are my rock and my fortress; therefore,
for Your name's sake, lead me and guide me.

PSALM 31:3

Are you serious about wanting God's guidance to become a personal reality in your life? The first step is to tell God that you know you can't manage your own life; that you need His help. Tell Him you promise to obey Him from now on, if He'll just make it clear to you what He wants you to do. . . .

The next step is to start reading the Bible . . . to get to know God for yourself. That will help you in getting His signals straight. . . . Get in the habit of reading a little bit of it the first thing in the morning or the last thing at night. Mark it up. Underline the places that seem to mean something special to you.

Not only will you begin to get an idea of how wonderful Jesus Christ is, but you will also find lots of helpful, specific principles of guidance that you can apply to the particular problems you want some answers on.

COINCIDENCE OR CONCERN?

I have raised him up in righteousness,
and I will direct all his ways.

ISAIAH 45:13

One day a stranger telephoned me saying that she would like to have a visit with me on the next afternoon. I made the date, forgetting about a conflicting dental appointment. By the time I remembered this, I realized that I had neglected to get the woman's telephone number. I had no idea how to get in touch with her. There was nothing to do but turn this little tangle over to God and ask Him to straighten it out for me.

About noon the next day, the lady telephoned. "I'm terribly sorry," she explained, "but I can't come this afternoon after all. My husband had to use the family car today."

There are those who would insist that such an incident is just a coincidence. But those of us who experience this kind of help over and over, know that it is God's hand in our lives.

THE LOVE GOD DEMANDS

Beloved, if God so loved us,
we also ought to love one another.

1 JOHN 4:11

Jesus' direction about love is clear: "You shall love the Lord your God with all your heart, with all your soul, with all your mind, and with all your strength. . . . You shall love your neighbor as yourself" (Mark 12:30–31). In all honesty, we know how little genuine love we bring to God even in moments of what is supposed to be worship, how feebly and selectively we love our neighbor. The love God demands can only be the gift of God. Yet He cannot give us that gift so long as bitterness and resentment have slammed shut the door of the heart and unforgiveness stands sentinel at the door lest love open and enter.

Forgiveness is the precondition to love.

GIFTS FROM GOD

By grace you have been saved through faith,
and that not of yourselves; it is the gift of God,
not of works, lest anyone should boast.

EPHESIANS 2:8–9

The natural balance of oxygen and nitrogen in the air we breathe is exactly right for men and animals. The law of gravity, which holds the world together, operates independently of us. And is man—little man who struts and fumes upon the earth—self-sufficient? Not at all. . . .

We want salvation from our sins and we yearn for eternal life. We think that we earn these things: Saul of Tarsus thought so too. Then we find out, as Paul did, that we cannot pile up enough good marks and merits to earn anything from God. No, salvation "is the gift of God: not of works, lest anyone should boast."

A BRIDGE OF RELATIONSHIP

*Let us pursue the things which make for peace
and the things by which one may edify another.*

ROMANS 14:19

The single most important element in any human relationship is real honesty—with oneself, with God, and with others, what Jesus called "walking in the light."

Let's admit it, we parents make mistakes in judgment, understanding, and behavior. There are times when we need to ask forgiveness of our children. In doing so, we build a bridge of relationship over which love can travel. Such honest confession demonstrates to the next generation a valuable tool for their own use later on. . . .

When we come to Jesus stripped of pretensions, with a needy spirit, ready to listen, He meets us at the point of need. He will undertake for us the task of untangling and cleansing at the emotional level. *He can make the difference in every human situation.*

THE PRAYER OF RELINQUISHMENT

He who does the will of God abides forever.

1 JOHN 2:17

A demanding spirit, with self-will as its rudder, blocks prayer. . . . The reason for this is that God absolutely refuses to violate our free will. Therefore, unless self-will is voluntarily given up, even God cannot move to answer prayer. . . .

Jesus' prayer in the Garden of Gethsemane is a pattern for us. "Dear Father, . . . Please let me not have to drink this cup. Yet it is not what I want, but what You want" (Luke 22:42, PHILLIPS). . . .

Even at the moment when Christ was bowing to the possibility of an awful death by crucifixion, He never forgot either the presence or the power of God. The Prayer of Relinquishment must not be interpreted negatively. It does not let us lie down in the dust of a godless universe and steel ourselves just for the worse. Rather it says: "This is my situation at the moment. I'll face the reality of it. But I'll also accept willingly whatever a loving Father sends."

PEOPLE ARE PRICELESS

This is My commandment,
that you love one another as I have loved you.

JOHN 15:12

My dad's life taught me the one thing that really matters—human relationships. The bonds that unite families and friends are not forged for a little while, they are for eternity. They stretch across every boundary of space and time. They twine and intertwine from one generation to another, weave and interweave, priceless beyond measure. They are something to be cherished, to be fought for, to be kept intact at all cost. People—with their fears and their foibles and their dreams. People—with their struggles toward faith, with the pain and the exaltation of their pilgrimage. People—with personalities that live on and on, growing, learning, loving, lending helping hands to others. *People*—that is what life is all about.

THE GOD-CENTERED PERSONALITY

Who is he who overcomes the world,
but he who believes that Jesus is the Son of God?

1 JOHN 5:5

The Egocentric Personality	The God-Centered Personality
"My will be done."	*"Thy will be done."*
Springs back slowly, painfully from disappointments.	Has capacity to rise above disappointments and use them creatively.
Trusts in material possessions for security.	Knows that security is in relationship to God, not things.
Indulges in self-pity when things go wrong.	Has objective resiliency when things go wrong.
Needs praise and publicity for good deeds.	Works well with others; can take second place.
Loves those who love her.	Can love the unlovely; has a feeling of oneness in God toward all humanity.

NO ONE BUT CHRIST

Jesus Christ is the same
yesterday, today, and forever.
HEBREWS 13:8

*S*ometimes I wonder how people can live at all without having met Christ. Other people fail us. Each of us has put a few people on pedestals even though we knew this is a dangerous thing to do—and always we discovered them human and fallible and disappointing. There are very few heroes left to our time. In whom can we finally believe?

In no one but Jesus Christ. He will never disappoint us, nor let us down. Turn the pages of your New Testament thoughtfully, and you will find that He is the only One who ever lived who met each crisis of life and of death head-on, with no flinching, no dodging, no compromise, yet with perfect love. If that seems too good to be true, try His friendship for yourself, now. He will be the same, always the same.

DOING GOD'S GOOD PLEASURE

Do not fear, little flock, for it is your
Father's good pleasure to give you the kingdom.

LUKE 12:32

Surely we have misunderstood Christianity if we think God wants us to obey Him reluctantly and fearfully—resisting, bucking, hating every step of the way. Jesus came to show us a new way by which God promises to work in us "both to will and to do of His good pleasure."

This means that God will bring about such a change in us that His plans and desires for us will be our delight. The secret of the will not only tells us how, but speeds us on our way with joy.

FAITH IS NOT A FEELING

If we know that He hears us, whatever we ask,
we know that we have the petitions that we have asked of Him.

1 JOHN 5:15

used to believe that faith had something to do with feeling. For example, when I had messed up some situation and had asked God for forgiveness, then I would peer inside myself to see if I felt forgiven. If I could locate such feelings, then I was sure that God had heard and had forgiven me. Now I know that this is an altogether false test of faith.

We would not be so foolish as to go to a railroad station, board the first car we saw, then sit down and try to feel whether or not this was the train that would take us where we wanted to go. Our feeling would obviously have no bearing on the facts. Yet I know now that at times my actions in the spiritual realm have been just that foolish.

GOD'S UNFAILING LOVE

He who believes in the Son of God has the witness in himself;
he who does not believe God has made Him a liar.

1 JOHN 5:10

We must let God bring deliverance. Almost always it takes longer than we think it should.

When we grow impatient and try a deliverance of our own, through friends or circumstances, we are taking God's work out of His hands.

John stated bluntly, "He who will not believe God, has made God a liar. . . ."

Believe what? Believe the consistent testimony in Scripture of the unfailing love and good will of our God, of His ability to help us, and of His willingness—indeed eagerness—to do so.

The adventure of living has not really begun until we begin to stand on our faith legs and claim—for ourselves, for our homes, for the rearing of our children, for our health problems, for our business affairs, and for our world—the resources of our God.

STRENGTHENING OUR FAITH

Faith comes by hearing and hearing by the word of God.

ROMANS 10:17

What can we do to strengthen our faith?

First, we cannot trust God until we know something about Him. The way to begin is by reading His word and thinking about it. The Bible acquaints us with the nature and character of God.

Second, faith is strengthened only as we ourselves exercise it. We have to apply it to our problems: poverty, bodily ills, bereavement, job troubles, tangled human relationships.

Third, faith has to be in the present tense—now. A vague prospect that what we want will transpire in the future is not faith, but hope.

Fourth, absolute integrity is necessary. We cannot have faith and a guilty conscience at the same time.

Fifth, the strengthening of faith comes through staying with it in the hour of trial. We should not shrink from tests of faith.

WISDOM FROM ABOVE

All the paths of the LORD are mercy and truth,
to such as keep His covenant and His testimonies.

PSALM 25:10

An American biographer needed to know some details about the life of a man who, during his lifetime, had lived in the British Isles. It looked as if all possible sources for the information had been exhausted. The writer specifically claimed God's promise, "If any of you lacks wisdom, let him ask of God, who gives to all liberally" (James 1:5).

Within a week, she received an invitation to have dinner with an English couple, whom she had met casually sometime before. During the evening, she spoke of her problem. Suddenly, her host interrupted. "You surely couldn't be speaking of Mr. ____, could you?"

The atmosphere in the room grew electric. "Yes—that's the very man. Why?"

"I worked beside him in the same engineering company for ten years. I knew him well!" Out of a million and a half residents of that city, God had led the writer straight to the door of the one man who could give her the information she needed.

GOD IN THE DETAILS

Let my prayer come before You;
incline Your ear to my cry.

PSALM 88:2

Often Christians ask, "Isn't it selfish to pray about the petty details of everyday living?"

No, not if we take Jesus' word on this. The total stream of our lives is made of the sum of just such details. When we ask for God's help only in the major decisions, we are admitting Him into a very small part of our lives.

Watch Jesus stride through the Gospels. He concerned Himself with peoples' health problems; with securing the money for Peter's tax; with the contents of one little boy's lunch box, so that hungry crowds could be fed; with a woman who lost one coin out of her wedding necklace; with one little lost sheep.

This is the message of the Bible from the beginning to end—not only that God cares about the individual, but that no detail of the individual's life is too small for His loving concern.

GOD'S PURPOSES

How precious are Your thoughts to me, O God!
How great is the sum of them.

PSALM 139:17

A typical correspondent asked, "What good purpose could God have had in taking Marie and leaving me alone here?"

The problem of evil—why a good God lets good people suffer—is forever with us. Certainly I have no pat answer. But we must remember that this old earth is enemy-occupied territory. Disease and death are of the enemy—not of a loving Father. Yet I do believe that when Marie was stricken God had some plan by which He could bring real good out of it.

Admittedly, it takes courage and no little faith to take the next constructive steps: hunt for the open door, the new creative purpose, rather than standing weeping before the closed door of grief. But God is the Creator. It isn't possible for Him to be negative. If we are to cooperate with His purposes (the only way of getting our prayers answered) we too must be creative and positive.

February

God insists that our walk be by faith,

not by a bird's-eye view of the whole terrain.

UNDER GOD'S LEADERSHIP

You shall love the Lord your God with all your heart,
with all your soul, with all your strength.

LUKE 10:27

Christianity, most of us think, is fine up to a point, so long as we can make it serve us. So long as it gives us peace of mind, settles some of the dust of our inner conflicts, makes us more likable people—well, fine! But of course this is peripheral stuff. This is interpreting Christianity as a rosewater philosophy to make a comfortable atmosphere of nice people. But nice people have no cutting edge. Nor have they any answers for the problems that beset our world.

We begin to see that no man is worthy to rule until he has been ruled: no man can lead well until he has given himself to leadership greater than his own. Even Jesus Christ was no exception. Repeatedly He said that He was not carrying out His own will, but the will of the One who sent Him.

PAINSTAKING PATIENCE

The everlasting God, the LORD, . . .
neither faints nor is weary.
His understanding is unsearchable.

ISAIAH 40:28

When Michelangelo accepted the commission to decorate the ceiling of the Sistine Chapel in the Vatican, he knew that the work would take many years. He would have to work in leisurely fashion, for he meant to create beauty for the inspiration of future generations.

As God works with each human life, His attitude is that of the artist who is creating a masterpiece—not just for time—but for eternity. No positive value ever built into any human personality is wasted. Therefore, God can afford to take infinite, painstaking trouble with each of us. He can be just as patient in molding us according to His perfect pattern, as we force Him to be.

God is very patient.

SELFLESS LOVE

God is love.

1 JOHN 4:16

On the human level, one of love's most obvious characteristics is unselfishness. The mother does not think of herself, but of the welfare of those she loves.

Since God is all love, . . . can His love be of a different caliber? The truth is that God is not only unselfish; He is *selfless*. His every thought, purpose, and plan since the beginning of time, has been for His children's welfare and happiness.

Yet many of us still view God as a jealous God, whose chief consideration is "His own glory." And out of this concept has grown fear—not faith and trust. We are afraid to release our affairs completely into God's hands, lest "His own glory" be at sharp variance with our good.

Faith is needed here, faith in the selfless love of God.

WILLING OUR WILLS

We know that we have passed from death to life,
because we love the brethren.

1 JOHN 3:14

I was a little girl when the evangelist, Gypsy Smith, Jr. came to Mississippi for a series of revival services. My most vivid recollections are of the dramatic reconciliations that took place in the services. Fellow townspeople and church officers—some of whom had not spoken to each other in years—knelt together before the altar and wept. It will not always be as dramatic as this, but there will always be reconciliations when the Spirit of God breaks through.

Dislike and hate are emotions. We do not have complete control over ourselves at an emotional level. But we can tell God that we are willing to forgive—that our wills give full assent to what God wants—and ask Him to deal with emotion. When we are sincere in praying, we find sooner or later our intense feelings are just dissolved by God.

PRIVILEGED PARTNERSHIP

You do not have, because you do not ask.

JAMES 4:2

Jesus assured us that our Father knows what things we have need of, before we ask Him (Matt. 6:8). Why, then, did Jesus bid us pray?

Because in giving us free will, God made the fulfilling of His plans for us dependent upon our glad and voluntary cooperation. Thus we have the privilege of being creators, in partnership with the Creator Himself.

God's creativity did not end with making the planet and man. He is and forever will be the Creator—constantly creating. This means that the whole emphasis of God's nature is always positive—never negative.

Yet most of our praying is negative. Analyze your own prayer requests. Are not most of them requests to get rid of something? Here, then, is one of the reasons for ineffectual and apparently unanswered prayers.

FORGIVE AND FORGET

Owe no one anything except to love one another,
for he who loves another has fulfilled the law.

ROMANS 13:8

God's love is not affected either in quality or in extent by our actions. But the idea that we can win God's love by good behavior is deeply rooted in us. That's why, when difficult circumstances come to us, we ask—like petulant children—"What have I *done* to deserve this?" Or when we see good things come to evil men, we are affronted and cry, "Why *should* the wicked prosper?"

There are Christians who resent the idea that the dying thief stole Paradise during the last few moments of earthly life and was admitted to God's love on the same basis as one who had served God during his entire life. . . .

We need to search our hearts for the right attitude. . . . Are we willing to forgive as Christ forgives, "remembering . . . sins . . . no more"?

GOD'S GOODWILL

Our help is in the name of the LORD,
who made heaven and earth.

PSALM 124:8

sks one elderly woman, "How could a loving God let . . . children become crippled with disease and young lives be snuffed out prematurely, while old people linger on and on?" It was a wistful question—and a haunting one.

How can you and I be sure what the will of God is? When Jesus assured us that God is good, did He mean just a spiritual benevolence? Or did He mean a goodness that includes unselfishness, thoughtfulness, compassion, and justice? . . .

Let us start at this lowest level of faith. Surely, we do not believe that God's goodwill toward His children is less than that of the least of our human friends.

FRIENDSHIP WITH THE FATHER

Oh, give thanks to the LORD, for He is good!
For His mercy endures forever.

PSALM 107:1

All human unhappiness stems from but two roots: (1) misunderstanding and misinformation about God, and (2) failure to obey God.

Even much of our disobedience grows out of our lack of knowledge. If we were truly acquainted with the Father, we would count obedience to Him our greatest privilege.

Therefore, to know God, as He really is—in His essential nature and character—is to arrive at a citadel of peace that circumstances may storm, but can never capture.

The unfolding of our friendship with the Father will be a never-ending revelation stretching on into eternity. Yet, for us, eternal life can begin here and now—as we embark on this most rewarding of all explorations.

MASTER AND LORD

I am One who bears witness of Myself,
and the Father who sent Me bears witness of Me.

JOHN 8:18

Jesus spoke as God would speak—with authority. His personality authenticated itself through the ring of authority. There was something incredible about the effect He had on His contemporaries.

One day two Galileans, Simon and Andrew, were fishing. Jesus came by and said, "Follow me." The two fishermen dropped all caution. Common sense was put aside. They actually left their nets and their business opportunities and followed the Master. It was a sort of divine madness. It is interesting to speculate on the reaction of their friends and relatives.

But the madness turned out to be wisdom; the Stranger became their Friend, their Lord.

DIVINE COMPASSION

Jesus . . . was moved with compassion for them,
because they were like sheep not having a shepherd.

MARK 6:34

The twelve apostles had returned from their preaching-healing mission. After hearing every glad detail, Jesus must have looked at them fondly as He said, "Now we'll go apart and rest. You need it." So they departed by boat for a secret retreat.

But the eager crowds got wind of it, and on the other side of the lake some ten thousand people awaited Jesus. Most of us would have felt annoyed, imposed upon. Not Jesus! There was only compassion in His heart for the jostling crowd. He "settled down" to preach and heal; then having pity on their creature-needs, He multiplied the loaves and fishes to feed them.

When the long day was over, He sent the weary apostles away secretly, covering their exit Himself. This was human thoughtfulness, the divine consideration of Jesus. He loves "plain folks" and is aware of our very human needs.

A BALANCE TO BUSYNESS

And when He had sent them away,
He departed to a mountain to pray.

MARK 6:46

The priority in Jesus' life was time for prayer with His Father. For this alone He would pull Himself away from those still unhealed or in need (Luke 4:42–43).
Jesus used prayer:

- for regular communion with God (Mark 1:35)
- to learn God's will—the prayer of decision (Luke 22:41–42)
- before making important decisions (Luke 6:12)
- for refreshments—to re-create His body and spirit, after being drained by an immense teaching and healing ministry (Mark 6:46–47)

Jesus can teach us the perfect balance between busyness and quietness, between service and prayer.

THE HEART'S DESIRE

*We all . . . are being transformed into the same image
from glory to glory, just as by the Spirit of the Lord.*

2 CORINTHIANS 3:18

When we allow the Spirit to guide us, He will concern Himself with our every desire and need—with how we use our time and spend our money. . . ;with what is happening to our children; with the health of our relationships with other people and with God. And, if our need is severe enough, the Holy Spirit will turn our lives upside down. . . .

How could any of us who have embarked on the pilgrimage that is Christianity do without Him? For we who long for something more, for strength and hope and wisdom beyond ourselves, discover to our joy that as the Comforter reveals Christ to us, in Him we have our heart's desire.

GOD IN OUR GRIEF

God will wipe away every tear from their eyes;
there shall be no more death, nor sorrow, nor crying.

REVELATION 21:4

Despite its universality, when sorrow comes to us, each of us is certain that no one has ever suffered such a keen sense of loss. And it is at that point that we can allow a poisonous self-pity to enter. Anger at God then often quickly follows.

But when we shut our heart against our friends and allow bitterness to creep in, we are, in a tragic way, insulating ourselves against the healing and re-energizing love of God.

I was saved from such isolation by a miracle of God's grace and by the loving church congregation that surrounded me. I use the word "miracle" because my basic nature has been that of fleeing encounters with people whenever possible. Yet somehow I was strengthened to will myself to return to the church the Sunday immediately following Peter's death, to sit in the pastor's pew as usual (though at times during the service I could not stop the tears), and thereafter to open wide the door of our manse-home to a procession of friends.

THE FATHERHOOD OF GOD

O LORD my God, You are very great:
You are clothed with honor and majesty.

PSALM 104:1

As the twentieth century has progressed, people have found the truth that God cares about each one of us increasingly difficult to believe. We need to be searchingly honest here. As children of a scientific age we have grown up indoctrinated with the concept of a mechanistic universe. Machines have all but taken over our everyday lives. The individual has come to feel lonely. Is anyone at home in the cosmos? Perhaps God *is* dead. And machines are not good company.

To loneliness is added helplessness. The individual feels like an all-but-worthless cog in the machinery of huge industrial bureaucratic nations. No wonder we find it a long leap from our century's framework of thinking to Jesus' sure teaching about the Fatherhood of God.

Yet whenever we are emboldened to accept and act on Jesus' revelation of the Fatherhood of God, always and always we find solid ground beneath our feet.

THE GREATEST ADVENTURE

Men always ought to pray and not lose heart.

LUKE 18:1

To Jesus, prayer was the greatest adventure of His life. Like Moses, on Mt. Sinai, in prayer He was stepping into the Presence of the Most-High God. God had thrilling secrets to share with Him, exciting new ideas, fresh concepts, so much to teach Him. Sometimes Jesus spent the entire night in prayer with His Father.

We, too, will have "chosen the better part" when we make prayer our priority. If the Resurrection has become a fact of experience to you and me, we, too, will approach prayer as sitting down at the feet of a living Lord to talk things over with Him. If we really believed this, would we not consider an hour a day with such a Teacher—a minimum, a joy, and our greatest privilege?

JOY FROM THE WELLS

Therefore with joy you will
draw water from the wells of salvation.

ISAIAH 12:3

God allows us to have disappointments, frustrations, or even worse because He wants us to see that our joy is not in such worldly pleasures as success or money or popularity or health or sex or even in a miracle-working faith. Our joy is in the fact that we have a relationship with God (Luke 10:20). Few of us ever understand that message until circumstances have divested us of any possibility of help except by God Himself.

It is a stripping process that we experience as we go on in the Christian life. . . . Once we have only God to depend on, . . . then we can *with joy* "draw water out of the wells of salvation" (Isa. 12:2–3). We draw out the precious water by rejoicing in Christ, our Deliverer, not in our circumstances or in anything about ourselves.

A BRIDGE OF BLESSING

I am the way, the truth, and the life.
No one comes to the Father except through me.

JOHN 14:6

When we look at our lives honestly, at our disappointment with ourselves, . . . at the frequent failures of our relationships with other people—we know there is a great gulf between our vulnerable humanness and the One who created us. And that gulf is like a broad and deep river.

For centuries people have been trying to throw bridges across that river; by sacrifices, . . . stringent rules, . . . by social reform. . . . But all these bridges fall short—and still the chasm yawns.

The fact is, it is impossible for human beings to throw out any bridge that will not fall short. Nor do we need to. The good news is that the bridge is already built! All we have to do is open our spiritual eyes, see it, and walk across it. It was for the specific purpose of spanning the chasm that God sent Jesus Christ into the world. The Christian message is that *He* is the bridge, the way of reconciliation.

COUNTING THE COST

*Whoever does not bear his cross
and come after Me cannot be My disciple.*

LUKE 14:27

Be careful what you promise God. He will take your promises at face value. "You'd better sit down and count the cost of being a disciple," warned Jesus, "before you promise anything" (Luke 18:28–35). What will the kingdom cost you? At the very least:

giving up other things, in order to have time for it (Luke 14:15),
putting Jesus ahead of every human relationship (Luke 14:26),
putting the kingdom ahead of possessions (Luke 14:33),
giving up all right to one's self (Mark 8:35),
obeying Jesus daily (Luke 9:23),
living to serve other people (John 13:13–16).

The kingdom is not for sentimentalists, but for those who mean business with God.

The LORD has done great things for us,
and we are glad.

PSALM 126:3

The Spirit delights in communicating Christ to us in everyday life. For instance, one morning about two years after Peter Marshall had his first heart attack, I was plagued by the insistent thought that I should learn to drive. Over a matter of months the idea kept coming back so persistently that I concluded this was the insistence of the Helper. Finally, Peter agreed to my taking driving lessons.

At the time of Peter's sudden death, I had been driving just long enough to have confidence to carry on. But if I had been forced to learn during the period of my emotional turmoil immediately following his death, I might never have attempted it. . . .

To me this seems proof, as only the Comforter can give it to us, that God exists, and that He cares about us. It is one way that we know, finally and forever, that we are loved and that this love can be expressed in simple, everyday ways straight from the unselfish heart of God.

THE LONG VIEW OF TIME

Do not forget this one thing,
that with the Lord one day is as a thousand years,
and a thousand years as one day.

2 PETER 3:8

Y ou know the words of the hymn "Take Time to Be Holy." . . . It does take time to be holy; it *does* take time to find the will of God. Usually it can't be done in the fifteen minutes just before you catch a train.

It *does* take time to think through our problems under Christ's tutelage. One of the attributes of God is that He seems so leisurely. Have you noticed that? He seems to have the view-point of all eternity. Somehow we still haven't succeeded in persuading Him to accept the speeded-up tempo of our lives. Often He seems to us to take so long—so terribly, maddeningly long—to answer our prayers.

A GLORIOUS PROMISE

Because I live, you will live also.

JOHN 14:19

With the calm assurance of one who knew He could conquer death, Jesus made that glorious promise to His disciples. In effect, Jesus was saying, "There is a life beyond the grave, and you will share it with me."

It is what we want to hear. We know that every moment of this strange and lovely life from dawn to dusk is a miracle. Somewhere, always, a flower is fading in the dusk. The incense that rises with the sun and the scents that die in the dark are all gathered up sooner or later into the solitary fragrance that is God; faintly, elusively that fragrance lingers over us all.

Sometimes we may not sense it in noisy streets, in clamorous cities, in busy offices, on crowded streetcars, or noisy restaurants. We seem to lose it.

That is why we have Easter services and sing Easter hymns, to catch again that strange haunting perfume like violet after an evening rain: "Because I live, you will live also."

GOD'S SENSE OF HUMOR

These things have I spoken unto you,
that My joy may remain in you,
and that your joy may be full.

JOHN 15:11

Can you think of anything more wonderful than that your God wants you to have joy? That doesn't mean our daily work will hold nothing unpleasant, nor that we won't know hard work. But who minds hard work so long as there is joy in the work?

Where does this idea come from that if what we are doing is fun, it can't be God's will? The God who made giraffes, a baby's fingernail, a puppy's tail, a crookneck squash, the Bobwhite's call, and a young girl's giggle has a sense of humor. Make no mistake about that!

GOD PREPARES THE PATH

If you do not forgive, neither will your
Father in heaven forgive your trespasses.

MARK 11:26

A member of a woman's family, over three thousand miles away, was angry at her. The woman tried to mend the rift through conciliatory letters but to no avail. Finally, even that communication stopped. The estrangement seemed final.

Then the woman decided that God wanted her to travel the three thousand miles for the specific purpose of getting the misunderstanding straightened out. Whenever we do our part, God does His. . . . At the end of the long journey, the two women met. There was no anger, only tears, softened hearts, and the birth of a new depth of understanding and friendship.

Said the women later, "It was a glorious answer to prayer. The result was worth the effort, a thousand times over."

Whenever we are willing, for Christ's sake, to go more than half way to mend a quarrel, it is as if God rushes joyously to prepare the way. It matters to Him!

A ZEST FOR LIFE

I come to You, [Father], . . . that they
may have My joy fulfilled in themselves.

JOHN 17:13

*H*ow long has it been since you have sung at your work because you couldn't help singing? Or sat by a friend and laughed until your stomach hurt and tears rolled down your cheeks? Or prayed with not one single request, just a prayer overflowing with spontaneous gratitude?

Of course Christ was "a man of sorrows and acquainted with grief." But that was in order that you and I need never again be defeated, nor resigned to the worst, nor bored, nor lack zest for life.

PRIVATE PRAYER

When you pray, go into your room,
and when you have shut your door, pray to your
Father who is in the secret place.

MATTHEW 6:6

There are various reasons why Jesus practiced secret prayer and asked us to follow His example. In our room with the door shut, we are not so likely to strut and pose and pretend as we are when another human being is present. We know that we cannot deceive God. Transparent honesty before Him is easier for us in isolation.

Then, too, there is the necessity of shutting out distractions—the doorbell, the telephone, . . . the children. God asks that we worship Him with our concentrated minds as well as with our wills and emotions. A divided and scattered mind is not effective.

THE EARTH IS THE LORD'S

You are a chosen generation,
a royal priesthood, . . . His own special people.

1 PETER 2:9

One of Christ's fundamental premises was that God is our Father who controls the earth's material resources. Simple words, but what a tremendous assertion! Most of us do not really believe this at all. Yet from cover to cover the Bible declares it:

The earth is the LORD's and all it's fullness . . . (Psalm 24:1).

My God shall supply all your need according to His riches . . . (Phil. 4:19).

If we *were* able to believe that we are children of a King and that He will supply every need, there would be no need of a greedy storing up of things. There would be no need to worry about money shortages, for worrying would be the sure sign that we did not believe God's ownership of the earth's resources. Furthermore, it would be wrong to have a "poverty complex," for to think ourselves paupers is to deny either the King's riches or our being His child.

THE SPIRIT OF TRUTH

When He, the Spirit of truth, has come,
He will guide you into all truth.

JOHN 16:12

*I*n His last talk with the eleven, Christ made it clear that they were to experience Him through the Spirit.... "Do not be frightened about my leaving you," Jesus told them, in effect. "It is actually to your advantage that I am going."

Then He outlined His plan. When He could no longer be with them physically, another ... would take His place. This One—the Helper—would be the continuation and extension of Christ's life on earth.... This had to be so, because there was more truth, much more, to be discovered.

This is the only plan whereby people through all the centuries could have fellowship with the risen Christ. Without the Spirit transmitting Christ's continuing presence to us, we would have no more than the memory and recorded words and deeds of any good man, such as St. Francis of Assisi, or Lincoln, or Gandhi.

KEEP PRESSING ON

Do not be afraid; only believe.

LUKE 8:50

Persistence on our part goes hand in hand with faith.

There seems to be a point in the application of faith, in any problem, when we have to keep pressing forward, in spite of seemingly immovable mountains and no response from God.

When Jesus promised us "knock, and the door will be opened to you," it is implied that there is a time when the door remains shut. This period of activity on man's part, with no seeming results, is the time when our faith often falters. But when faith persists, it is rewarded by an act of initiative on God's part. It is He who opens the door to our needs and solves our problems.

March

No problem is any match

for the Lord God Almighty!

POSITIVE PRAYER

Ask, and you will receive, that your joy may be full.

JOHN 16:24

There was once an unhappy family. The home was full of tension because of an aunt's nagging and fault-finding with the children. The mother prayed about this almost constantly. Her method was to ask God to take away the relative's critical attitude. In praying thus, her own criticism of her aunt increased. Nothing seemed to happen in spite of all her prayers.

Then someone suggested that she just ask that the family have fun together—nothing more. The mother accepted the challenge . . . and her prayer was bountifully answered.

In the first kind of prayer, the woman had been negative. She was asking to get rid of something. Get-rid-of-prayers are petty prayers; God cannot be petty.

In the second type of prayer, the woman used her positive request as an open door through which God could come into the situation. She and God became partners in creating one more small area of light and joy in the world.

OVERFLOWING JOY

My soul shall be joyful in my God;
for He has clothed me with the garments of salvation.

ISAIAH 61:11

*J*esus drew men and women into the Kingdom by promising them two things: first, trouble— in the sense of hardship, danger, even misunderstandings; and second, joy. But what curious alchemy is this that He can make even danger and hardship seem joyous? He understands some things about human nature that we grasp only dimly: few of us are really challenged by the promise of soft living, by an emphasis on me-first or by a life of easy compromise.

So Christ still asks for the total surrender and then promises His gift of full, overflowing joy.

VICTORY OVER DEATH

*The wages of sin is death, but the gift
of God is eternal life in Christ Jesus our Lord.*

ROMANS 6:23

esus went to His cross as the willing agent of the divine plan. Nevertheless, His agony in Gethsemane shows us that humanly He shrank from the torturing hours ahead. All His growing-up years in Nazareth He had seen crucifixions. . . . He could scarcely have helped seeing the crucifixion by Varrus, Prefect of Syria, of 2000 rioters after the death of Herod the Great. The field full of 2000 crosses would have made an indelible impression on any sensitive boy. How well He knew that the nails used in crucifixion (square, one-third inch on each side) were real enough, as real as the pain and the agonizing thirst, the cramps, and the ultimate asphyxiation. Even so He considered that "for this cause I was born, . . ." (John 18:37). Therefore, He was "obedient unto death."

The victory was God's, for on the third day life poured back into the dead and mutilated body of Jesus. The crucifixion and resurrection are history's watershed.

FRUIT IN MY LIFE

By this My Father is glorified,
that you bear much fruit; so you will be My disciples.

JOHN 15:8

The Vinedresser is at work on me. Decisive pruning is taking place (John 15:2). He means to have fruit in my life—or else! I have already, at several points in the past, given Him permission for this—though so often at the time I pray in such a manner, I little realize to what extent "praying is dangerous business."

Well, Lord, I'm not there quite yet; I can't quite grasp the joy and gladness and delight in the midst of pruning. But it is a great comfort to be able to lean back on Your sovereignty and omnipotence, knowing that You are the One who chose me and that You planted me (vs. 16). That means that the results of Your gardening and tending *have* to be good!

GOD'S POWER, NOT MINE

"Not by might nor by power, but by My Spirit," says the LORD of hosts.

ZECHARIAH 4:6

I've discovered a truth this morning in the twenty-first chapter of John.

Peter and four others fished all night and caught nothing. As morning came Jesus arrived on the beach and called to them: "Have you any food?"

When they replied "No," Jesus told them to cast their nets on the right side of the boat and they could "find some."

They did as He suggested and landed 153 fish, most of them large ones!

The message to me: I can expend all my energy for many hours on a task, using my best resources, and produce exactly nothing. A zero. All because I'm doing it in my own strength and not with the help of my Lord.

THE GOODNESS OF THE LORD

I had fainted, unless I had believed to see
the goodness of the LORD in the land of the living.

PSALM 27:13

The family doctor had been to see a sick child. When the minister came, he found the mother torn with uncertainty as to whether it was God's will that her child recover.

Gently, the minister asked, "When the doctor came, did you stop him in the lower hall, to question him as to whether he was willing to try to cure Barbara?"

"No—of course not." . . .

"Then would you attribute less goodwill to God than to your family physician?"

Light broke through for this mother and she was able to pray with faith in the certainty of God's love. . . . Admittedly, there is a deep mystery here. Sometimes, our prayers are not answered as we wish. Yet, we can be sure that the solution does not lie in questioning the goodness of our God; for, in that direction, lies only utter darkness.

GRACE TO THE HUMBLE

Be clothed with humility,
for God resists the proud,
but gives grace to the humble.

1 PETER 5:5

have begun to see that *humiliation* is simply the basic understanding and admission that God is truly God—sovereign and omnipotent—and that we are His creations, limited so long as we are in the flesh, by our humanity.

Humiliation is dropping the born-and-bred-in-arrogance of our creatureliness and bowing low in worship before our Creator.

Jesus Christ, ever our Way-Shower, is our example here. Listen to His ringing declaration about our neediness: "Apart from Me you can do nothing" (John 15:5, RSV).

THE COMFORTER HAS COME!

It is best for you that I go away,
for if I don't, the Comforter won't come.
If I do, he will—for I will send him to you.

JOHN 16:7, TLB

These are the blessed, blessed functions of the Holy Spirit as described by Jesus Himself:

Comforter (He brings solace to all our hurts)

Counselor (the source of all wisdom)

Helper (He lifts us over obstacles)

Advocate (Our personal lawyer to "take us on" and plead our case)

Intercessor (How we all need *that!*)

Strengthener (He gives us the vitality we need)

GOD REALLY DOES LOVE US

If we ask anything according to His will,
He hears us. And if we know that He hears us, whatever we ask,
we know that we have the petitions that we have asked of Him.

1 JOHN 5:14–15

I have found through the experiences in my life that our all-too-human tendencies to ask "Why?" have gotten me nowhere at all. I am certain that other Christians through the centuries have found exactly the same thing. Perhaps one reason for this is that God requires us to have faith in the fact that He really is an all-loving God in Whom there is no darkness and that He really does love us. It is only after we are willing to stand on that and deposit our trust in His love that we begin to get some answers. Oh, how I am looking forward to that time when I can meet the living Lord in person. I have so many questions now I'd like to present to Him. I wonder if they will still be important when I see Him.

HEALTHY HELPLESSNESS

*I can do all things
through Christ who strengthens me.*

PHILIPPIANS 4:13

Our helplessness can be a healthy sign. This is always a good place to begin a task that seems completely impossible. We are all helpless to change someone else's heart, or our own. We're helpless to manufacture love. We're helpless to mend our own bodies. The greatest physicians and surgeons can only medicate, cut, and repair—in the end nature must do the healing. But there is Someone who makes possible what seems completely impossible.

Jesus put it succinctly: Without *Me*, you can do nothing (John 15:5).

GOD IN EACH MOMENT

Truly, truly, I say to you,
the Son can do nothing of His own accord
but what He sees the Father doing.

JOHN 5:18, RSV

If Jesus, with His continual awareness of the Father's luminous presence and guidance could do or say nothing without His Father, then how much greater is our need for Him? . . .

What this means is that each day I must find a way to walk with Him, talk with Him. And not just during my morning prayer time, but during the entire day. I will begin my work with Him there beside me at my desk. "Jesus, how do I start writing this chapter?"

Jesus will be there at the lunch table, when I lie down to rest, when I answer letters with my secretary, when Len and I take our walks together, when I listen to music and sew. There is a way to bring Him into everything I do.

PERSONALITY POWER

Take heed that you do not do your
charitable deeds before men, to be seen by them.
Otherwise you have no reward from your Father in heaven.

MATTHEW 6:1

any of us are living scattered and impoverished lives. The reason is that when we perform a good deed, we proudly advertise, display it, and collect the credit. Unworthy or bad deeds, we hide. The "credit" (really debit) of the bad acts stays with us, accumulates. Thus our personalities are left on the debit side. Mentally and spiritually we remain chronically bankrupt.

But if we would really like to become fulfilled and productive persons, we must reverse the process. That is, we must divest ourselves of weaknesses, faults, and sins by confessing them. All kindness and good deeds, we must keep secret. The result will be an inner reservoir of personality power.

TO GLORIFY GOD

To God, alone wise,
be glory through Jesus Christ forever.

ROMANS 16:27

How do we find *the glory that comes from the one God?* I believe it comes through obedience to Him. This is not easy because it means we have to establish communication with the Lord through daily prayer. I do this by beginning each day with a time of reading (usually from the Bible) and prayer in which I ask for His guidance. From then on during the day if something pops into my mind—perhaps a simple household chore or the name of a person to call or write—then I stop what I'm doing and take the action that He seems to want. If I'm confused, I'll ask Him again about it. If still confused—and the action suggested seems a bit far out—I'll check the guidance with my husband, mother, or close friend, and together we'll pray for further illumination. But I've learned that when I disregard these "inner nudges," I do so at my own loss.

THE FACETS OF FAITH

Without faith it is impossible to please Him.

HEBREWS 11:6

Almost always Jesus ascribed His miracles to the individual's faith. "Have faith in God!" He admonished us. But what is faith?

Light passing through a prism, is broken up into its component parts. Just so, faith as Jesus lived it, always had these facets:

- Faith that God loves the individual—even me (Luke 12:6–7)
- Faith that God's power can break through to my difficulty (Mark 9:23)
- Faith in God's willingness to deal with my specific problems (Matt. 7:9–11)
- Faith that God wants to act on my behalf *now* (Mark 10: 52)

STRONGHOLD OF TRUTH

The weapons of our warfare are not carnal
but mighty in God for pulling down strongholds.

2 CORINTHIANS 10:4

he picture comes to my mind of a strong, fortified castle atop a steep hill with precipitous cliffs all around. Deep inside a man or woman is held in chains, a prisoner. The stronghold is heavily guarded. *This* is Satan's stronghold. The above passage tells us the weapons of our spiritual warfare are mighty and powerful to pull down and demolish such strongholds.

But Scripture also tells me that Satan's strongholds are delusions, unreal, lies. . . . The only real stronghold is Jesus Himself and the truth He stands for: *The LORD is good, a stronghold in the day of trouble; and He knows those who trust in Him* (Nahum 1:7).

A BOUQUET OF COMPLIMENTS

Let us come before His presence with thanksgiving;
let us shout joyfully to Him with psalms.

PSALM 95:2

Corrie ten Boom, sturdy Dutch survivor of Nazi concentration camps, and known for the book and the motion picture *The Hiding Place*, was once asked how she handled compliments.

Corrie, known to be impatient of all who tried to elevate her to instant sainthood, made a clucking noise followed by a snort. "Why, compliments are just like being handed flowers," was her quick response. "I keep gathering them through the day—one or two roses here, a few tulips there, a carnation or so, some daisies—a few stems here, a few stems there.

"Then at the end of the day, with a feeling of total gratitude I just hand the entire bouquet of compliments over to the One who really deserves them. A bouquet of flowers for *You,* Lord. They all belong to You.'"

NOT OF THE WORLD

Because you are not of the world,
but I chose you out of the world, therefore the world hates you.

JOHN 15:19

Jesus told us what will happen if we give God's will first place in our lives. He promised us three things. The first thing we do not like at all. He explained in a thoroughly realistic manner that if we were of the world, the world would love its own. But because we are not of the world, but chosen out of the world, the world is not going to approve of us; . . . it may even persecute or hate us (John 15:19). This cost must be counted. It is a real cost, and Jesus would not deceive us on that.

But then He goes on to give us the pluses that we shall have if we put God's will first in our lives. The first plus is that faith or belief—a belief rooted not in theory, but in experience—will be given to us.

Secondly, Jesus told us that only in God's will would we have real freedom.

HEALING HURTS

Neither do I condemn you: go and sin no more.

JOHN 8:11

*J*esus is all compassion. He never berates us. He sees sin as much broader than mere moral or spiritual delinquency. Sin is any deed or memory that hampers or binds human personality.

Is there anything in our past of which we are ashamed? Do we have painful memories? Do any sordid mental images rise sometimes to haunt us? Is there a locked junk room in the depths of our beings, into which we have crammed certain people and experiences to try to forget them?

If so, then we need the healing forgiveness of Jesus Christ. He alone can sweeten sordid memories and take the sting out of deep hurts. We get that cleansing by going to Him and telling Him everything. We must unlock every door and throw open every window in the depths of our personality.

GOD THE FATHER

I will be to Him a Father and He shall be to Me a son.

HEBREWS 1:5

n watching Jesus, what did His disciples learn about God?

The most obvious thing they observed was the daily intimacy of Jesus' relationship with His Father. At first this must have puzzled them. For always He appeared to be listening to a Voice beyond Himself. There is no record of His ever having argued with anyone about the existence of God; this was fact. Also there was no doubt that God was always present to help, to guide, to succor.

Jesus acted as if there was never any question of the Father's willingness to supply all needs—even such material ones as appeasing hunger. God was concerned about men's bodies along with their souls: Divine love delighted in dispelling pain, in restoring sanity, in straightening crooked limbs and opening blind eyes. . . . Jesus said that in heaven there was an instant readiness to forgive and great joy over finding the lost.

HOUSECLEANING OF THE HEART

*If you do not forgive men their trespasses,
neither will your Father forgive your trespasses.*

MATTHEW 6:15

ying in bed through a lengthy illness proved a valuable time for some much-needed housecleaning of my heart. Through agonizing days I made methodical notes on all the ignoble traits and deeds of my past. . . . Having confessed every wrong that had surfaced to my conscious mind, I then specifically . . . prayed that God would see to it that any residue of debris in my subconscious would eventually come to light. Or that He would deal with anything there by pouring His cleansing and healing Spirit into my mind.

In subsequent months . . . I became aware of a compartment in my being in which I had locked certain persons whom I disliked. They could go their way; I would go mine. But now Christ seemed to be standing by the locked door saying, "That isn't forgiveness. It won't do. No closed doors are allowed. The Kingdom of God is the kingdom of right relationships."

SOMETIMES GOD SAYS "NO"

We have known and believed the love that God has for us.

1 JOHN 4:16

Sometimes as parents we grant our children their way, just because we lack the necessary discipline to say "no". This is really refined parental selfishness. We cannot bear for our children to doubt our love for them—even temporarily. This would impinge our ego. Our desire for the goodwill of our child is greater than the quality of our love, greater even than our determination to do the highest things.

God's love is free of this ego and selfishness. There are times when He does say "no" to us. He is willing to run the risk of us misunderstanding, is always disciplined, and hence his is a powerful love.

KNOWING GOD

The works that I do in My Father's name,
they bear witness of Me. . . . I and My Father are one.

JOHN 10:25, 30

A college professor—a man of unusual intellectual honesty—went to talk to his local minister. "I have no trouble believing in God," he said, "but I'm puzzled as what to believe about Christ. Can you help me?"

"What do you believe about God?" asked the minister.

"Well, that He's good, living, has all power . . ."

"All true," smiled the minister. "I'll tell you how to resolve this. Take a pencil and paper; go off by yourself; put down all the specific things you believe about God. Then go back over that list and think through the *source* of those ideas."

The professor tried this. He was thorough and honest. When next he saw the minister, he said, "I see now why you asked me to make that list. I discovered that every idea I had about God really came from Jesus. I see now how Jesus alone reveals the nature of God."

SELF AT THE CENTER?

Do you not know that friendship
with the world is enmity with God?

JAMES 4:4

How on earth can you believe while you are forever looking for one another's approval and not for the glory that comes from the one God? (John 5:41–44, *PHILLIPS*) I've spent hours pondering that verse because I think it cuts to the heart of the problem of ineffective faith, of missing out on the joy and power that comes from an all-out relationship with Jesus Christ.

One obstacle to such a relationship is the importance we place on the approval of our friends and associates. Are we willing to risk their approval by taking a stand for our beliefs? . . .

The question arises—why is it obnoxious to God that we make the approval of our peer group the criterion of our conduct? The answer I receive is that when we make our decisions this way, *self* is at the center of our life instead of God. And this self-centeredness will block us from God's power and love.

HAPPINESS AND FULFILLMENT

By this we know love,
because He laid down His life for us.

1 JOHN 3:16

have been surprised to find that so many people honestly do not believe that God wants our happiness and fulfillment. We've heard all our lives that God is love, but we insist on spiritualizing this. Many Christians have been taught that God's love is different from ours—not the kind His creatures understand. Deeply imbedded in our consciousness is the idea that God is primarily interested in our spiritual and moral rectitude; therefore, most of what He requires of us will be about as welcome as castor oil.

Of course God is concerned about our growing into mature believers. And the God I know sometimes asks difficult things of us, it is true. But His will also includes a happiness here on earth abundant enough to float every difficulty.

EXTRAVAGANT FAITH

We walk by faith, not by sight.

2 CORINTHIANS 5:7

During His ministry on earth Christ had one consistent message to the faint-hearted: "All things are possible to him who *believes*" (Mark 9:23). "Have faith in God. . . . Whatever things you ask when you pray, *believe* that you receive them, and you will have them" (Mark 11:22, 24). "If you have faith and *do not doubt*, . . . if you say to this mountain, 'Be removed and be cast into the sea', it will be done" (Matt. 21:21).

These may seem audacious, extravagant statements to us, but they weren't to Jesus. Through miracle after miracle He showed us what He could do *through His faith* in the Father. Then He challenged His disciples down through the ages to do the same.

LIFE IN THE FULLEST SENSE

Of Him you are in Christ Jesus, who became
for us wisdom from God—and righteousness
and sanctification and redemption.

1 CORINTHIANS 1:30

In this verse Paul gives us not only powerful teaching on humility, but a clear statement of the five things we receive when we invite Jesus into our lives:

1. Wisdom from God
2. Righteousness (thus making us upright and putting us in right standing with God)
3. Consecration (making us pure and holy)
4. Redemption (providing our ransom from the eternal penalty for sin)
5. Life (in the fullest, most vital sense)

NO GREATER LOVE

I in them and you in Me; . . .
that the world may know that You have sent Me,
and have loved them as You have loved Me.

JOHN 17:23

God would scarcely give fathers and mothers a greater capacity for loving their children than He Himself has for loving all His children. I suggest . . . that God would not have bothered to create father-love and mother-love in the first place, if He Himself did not have it in great abundance. . . .

How grieved God must be that any of His children should cower before Him in fright. . . . How often we attribute emotions and deeds to Him that we would ascribe only to the most depraved of human minds. Probably no personality in the universe is so maligned as that of the Creator.

MORE THAN WE ASK

To Him who is able to do exceedingly
abundantly above all that we ask or think . . . be glory.

EPHESIANS 3:20–21

If we think we'll never be able to summon the faith to seek specific answers to prayer, we're right. However, those saints who have had the most experiences here on earth tell us that God uses our most stumbling, faltering faith-step as the open door to His doing for us "more than we ask or think."

We first decide to ask His help with some small immediate need. Our asking is like stepping into a tiny anteroom. Taking a hesitant step forward, we discover that the anteroom leads into the King's spacious reception hall. To our astonishment, the King Himself comes forward to meet us, offering a gift so momentous as to be worthy only of the King: a lifetime gift of friendship with the Lord of Glory.

A BLUNT QUESTION

You do not have because you do not ask.

JAMES 4:2

James had learned the necessity of asking from Jesus Himself. One day the band of twelve traveling with the Master met two blind men who cried, "O Lord, Son of David, have pity on us!"

Jesus silenced the men's singsong chant with the blunt question, "What do you want me to do for you?"

The directness of the question shocked the beggars out of their self-pitying, pious stance. "Lord, we want our eyes opened," they pleaded. . . .

So Jesus touched the eyes of each beggar in turn, and immediately their eyes received sight. This was Jesus' way . . . "Tell me exactly what you want," He was always saying. "Talk to Me. *Ask* Me."

LOVE FREELY GIVEN

Let not mercy and truth forsake you; . . .
write them on the tablet of your heart.

PROVERBS 3:3

Surely there is a difference (and it is not just a quibble) between God's ideal will and His permissive will. Thus, in my case, I cannot believe that it was God's ideal will that Peter Marshall die at forty-six. But given a certain set of circumstances—among them Peter's inherited physique, so fine that he was inclined to overtax it—God had an alternate plan by which He could bring unimagined good even out of early death. . . .

By giving humans freedom of will, the creator has chosen to limit His own power. He risked the daring experiment of giving us the freedom to make good or bad decisions, to live decent or evil lives, because God does not want the forced obedience of slaves. Instead, He covets the voluntary love and obedience of children who love Him for Himself.

COMMISSIONED FOR CHRIST

He who believes in Me,
the works that I do he will do also;
and greater works than these he will do....

JOHN 14:12

esus' meaning was unmistakable. His "works" were the forgiving of sins, the healing of bodies and minds, the restoration of whole personalities.

Either Jesus was mistaken, when He thought that His disciples down the centuries could do even greater works than He had done, or—we are failing Him.

Our commission is quite specific. We are to be His witnesses to all nations (Acts 11:8) by:

- preaching the gospel (Mark 16:15)
- teaching and baptizing (Matt. 28:18–20) . . .
- laying hands on the sick as Jesus' representatives (Mark 16:18)

For us, as His disciples, to refuse any part of this commission, frustrates the love of Jesus Christ, the Son of God.

April

Give me the gift of eyes that see,

of ears that hear what God is saying to me.

BROWSING OR BELIEVING?

I will put My trust in Him.

HEBREWS 2:12

*I*n order to make sure we are not retreating from the tension of faith, it is helpful to ask ourselves as we pray, "Do I really expect anything to happen?" This will prevent us from going window-shopping in prayer. At times window-shopping can be enjoyable; but there it ends. It costs nothing. We are just looking, have no intention of buying anything, so we bring nothing home to show for the hours of browsing. Too many of our prayers—private and public—are just browsing amongst possible petitions, not down to cases at all. We expect nothing from our prayers except perhaps a feeling of well-being.

One veteran prayer warrior, John R. Rice, expressed it bluntly in *Asking and Receiving:* "Prayer is not a lovely sedan for a sight-seeing trip around the city. Prayer is a truck that goes straight to the warehouse, backs up, loads, and comes home with the goods."

TROUBLES TURNED TO TRIUMPHS

God is able to make all grace abound toward you,
that you, . . . may have an abundance for every good work.

2 CORINTHIANS 9:8

Not only is God always beside us in trouble, identified with our suffering, but He can also make everything—even our troubles and sorrow— "work together for good" (Rom. 8:28).

How many times I have received letters from readers . . . who marveled at how God accomplished this in my case. Such was the case with this letter from New Zealand: "How I wish I might have heard Dr. Marshall preach! We are so far away here in New Zealand, I would never have known about him at all, had it not been for *A Man Called Peter*. And now, to think that he is preaching to more people than ever today through that book."

This is not to say that God willed Peter's death in order that He might bring about a widened ministry. Rather that given his death, God could turn even that to good.

CARING COMPASSION

As many as touched Him were made well.

MARK 6:56

The Gospels reveal a divine impatience in Jesus. With Him, *now* was always the appointed time to get rid of the devil's work.

One Sabbath day, while teaching in a synagogue, Jesus saw a woman who was bent double. She had been in that sad state for eighteen years.

The woman did not ask Jesus to heal her; He took the initiative. . . . He was not willing to wait even a few hours until the Sabbath should be over, to release the woman. Thereby, He incurred the wrath of the Jewish leaders.

Jesus was unwilling to tolerate an instant longer that necessary any negative, binding, degrading quality in human life.

A DOOR OF HOPE

You are my hope; O LORD God;
You are my trust from my youth.

PSALM 71:5

ooking back, I can see that the most exciting events of my life have all risen out of trouble.

The three-year illness that forced me into a spiritual exploration that revolutionized my personal Christian living; then the deep dale of Peter Marshall's death and the door that eventually opened into a writing career for me. In fact, the deeper the difficulty, the more dramatic the creativity God has brought from it.

Easter comes each year to remind us that this truth is eternal and universal. On Good Friday long ago Evil surged to its climax on a hill shaped like a skull. But the empty tomb of Easter morning says to you and me, "Of course you'll encounter trouble. But behold a God of power who can take any evil and turn it into a door of hope."

WILLING GOD'S WILL

Then He said, "Behold, I have come to do Your will, O God."

HEBREWS 10:9

It is not enough . . . to experiment with being obedient to God. It has to be a total decision in one's will. And if you read through the New Testament, it is obvious to His friends and enemies alike that Jesus had but one criterion of action—the will of His Father for Him. They said of Him once, "Teacher, we know you are straight in what you say and teach, you do not look to human favor but teach the way of God honestly" (Luke 20:21, MOFFATT).

Christ obviously expected every one of His disciples in that day (and in this) to have the same standard of action. "What does God want me to do today? Am I willing, if necessary, to be a fool for His sake?"

FULL FELLOWSHIP

Love your neighbor as yourself.

MARK 12:31

Our relationship with other people is of primary importance to God. Because God is love, He cannot tolerate any unforgiveness or hardness in us towards any individual. God commands that we forgive regardless who is to blame.

The air around us is full of electricity. But that electricity cannot be harnessed to light our homes and work for us unless it is grounded.

Just so, the universe is full of the power of God. But that power cannot become available to transform lives and obtain answers to prayer, without God's ground wire. God's ground wire is our relationship with our fellow-man.

God reaches down to hold my hand. It is He who, in every instance, takes the initiative. With my other hand, He bids me touch the lives of others. Only as both connections are made, can I have full and satisfying fellowship with the God of love.

GOOD NEWS, INDEED!

While we were still sinners, Christ died for us.

ROMANS 5:8

A young man in the armed services had long ignored God. Finally, the time came when he sorely needed God's help. The boy was refreshingly honest. "When things were going well with me," he said, "I just ignored God. Now, only the lowest kind of worm would come crawling back to ask for help. Nobody could deserve help less than I do. I just can't be that kind of sponger."

The boy's minister explained to him that nothing he could ever do would be good enough to "deserve" God's help. All of us, sooner or later, must come to God on His terms—not on ours! And God's terms are our empty hands and what Christ did for each of us on a hill outside of Jerusalem.

The young man finally saw the point. "Why that's wonderful! Why didn't somebody tell me this before? That's good news."

It is indeed good news!

MATURING MOMENT BY MOMENT

But if we hope for what we do not see,
we eagerly wait for it with perseverance.

ROMANS 8:25

Once we recognize our need for Jesus, then the building of our faith begins; . . . a daily, moment-by-moment life of absolute dependence upon Him for everything.

Often, as the practical needs of our everyday life are met we *know* that He is with us, that His power is real, that He hears us, and that He responds more gloriously than we could have believed.

At this point, we can pray, believing that a husband's cold heart will melt because Jesus will be doing the melting. When an impossible situation confronts us, we can pray, knowing that to Jesus nothing is impossible.

The only prerequisite you need in every emergency, small and large, is simply to tell Jesus, "I don't know the answer, Lord, or what to do. You tell me."

And He will.

INSTRUCTIONS FOR LIFE

If you walk in My statutes and keep
My commandments, . . . I will give peace in the land.

LEVITICUS 26:3–6

he Book of Leviticus contains an amazing record of the detail to which a loving God will go to help His children. Germs were discovered about 1877 by Louis Pasteur. Yet about 1250 B.C. God gave detailed instructions for cleanliness, careful quarantine, and control of communicable diseases.

In our enlightened century, Americans began to take crop rotation and soil conservation seriously about 1908. Yet, between eleven to twelve centuries before Christ, God showed men how to farm, so that the soil would never be depleted. . . .

Can we believe that God cares less today? Or that—if we as a nation would turn to Him—He would not give us just as far-advanced and detailed a plan for the monumental needs of our time?

ABSOLUTE OBEDIENCE

*I do not seek My own will
but the will of the Father who sent Me.*

JOHN 5:30, PHILLIPS

here is sharp necessity for giving Christ absolute obedience. The devil bids for our complete self-will as over against God's will. To whatever extent we give this self-will the right to be master, we are, to that extent, giving Satan a toehold. We are going the way he goes, saying "yes" to Satan and "no" to God. . . .

Jesus is not impressed by our lip service—"What is the point of calling me Lord, Lord, without doing what I tell you to do? . . ." (Luke 6:46) Only when the fascination that many of us feel for Jesus becomes a discipleship of obedience are we fully received into His family (Luke 8:21).

PRECIOUS IN HIS SIGHT

You must let little children come to me,
and you must never stop them.

MATTHEW 19:13, PHILLIPS

ne day a man named Jairus came to Jesus for help. His only child, a little girl of twelve, was dying. Would the Master heal her? Jesus did not hesitate. Of course He would! But the crush of the crowd was suffocating. Before Jesus could get there, word was brought to the distraught father that his child had died.

The scene that follows is full of tenderness and is typical of Jesus' every contact with children. There is even the little human touch. After raising her from death Christ instructed the family, "Get her something to eat now. She'll be hungry!"

Some of the gentlest words Christ ever spoke were on behalf of children. And one of the sternest warnings He ever gave . . . was in defense of them (Matt. 18:5–6). The world's children are very precious to Jesus.

BOTHERING THE FATHER?

Let the beauty of the LORD our God be upon us,
and establish the work of our hands for us.

PSALM 90:17

Have we any right to bother God with the details of daily life?

We should be wary of any interpretation of religion so self-centered that it continually seeks, "What can my faith do for me today?" And we should have a healthy fear of making our God too small. (They are right who see Him as the God of history with far-flung designs for man's destiny.)

Yet the fact remains the Jesus added for us another dimension to the nature of His Father. "By all means you *should* bother the Father with the details of life," Jesus seems to say in so many places in the Gospels. He was constantly "bothering the Father" with the practicalities of life—with people's health problems, . . . with supper for a crowd of hungry listeners, with the wine running out at a wedding reception.

DEEP-FLOWING JOY

Though now you do not see Him,
yet believing, you rejoice with joy inexpressible and full of glory.

1 PETER 1:8

What God wants for us is exactly what every thoughtful parents wants for his child—the pure, deep-flowing joy that springs out of maturity and fulfillment.

That God is like this, each of us must discover for ourselves. There is only one difficulty. The discovery comes second, the act of will first. The order of events can never be reversed: action on our part, that is, the decision to hand our life over to God and the promise of obedience; then, and only then comes understanding and the unfolding knowledge of the character of God.

CREATOR AND CREATURE

He who has seen Me has seen the Father.

JOHN 14:9

A scientist stood studying an anthill. Whenever his shadow fell across the hill, the terrified ants scurried in all directions.

"My problem," mused the scientist, "is how to reassure these tiny creatures of my goodwill. If only I could speak to them! But that would be possible only if somehow, I could become one of them, and speak their language."

This was God's problem too. Far greater than the chasm between ants and man, is the chasm between the Creator and the created. . . .

And so, God solved this problem in the Incarnation. At a specific point in time, Jesus broke into history. He became one of us. He lived among us; He spoke our language. If we want to know what the Father is like, we have but to look at Jesus.

OUR GREATEST GOOD

My thoughts are not your thoughts,
nor are your ways My ways.

ISAIAH 55:8

*A*t would seem to us that if ever the free will of wicked men—sundered from and at cross-purpose with the will of God—was in control, it was at the execution of Jesus Christ by crucifixion.

"Not so," was Jesus' assertion. Never for an instant during the acting out of that drama did God abdicate as sovereign Ruler. Christ made this point over and over. . . .

The powers of darkness in control? It only appeared so. Long before Passion week, Jesus was explaining, "My Father loves me, because I lay down my life, that I might take it again. No one takes it from me, but I lay it down of Myself" (John 10:17–18).

Thus even the events that swept Christ toward the cross had been woven into a plan for the greatest good of mankind.

MOUNTAIN REMOVING

If you have faith and never doubt, . . .
even if you say to this mountain, "Be taken up
and cast into the sea," it will be done.

MATTHEW 21:21

ike a trumpet-call, Christ's constant reiteration for the need of faith sounds through the gospel narratives. Clearly, He saw all the evil . . . inherent in life. All mountains of evil, He asserted, were the work of the devil (Luke 10:18; 13:16; 1 John 3:8). Moreover, He had come to earth to show us that the Father does not want us to spiritualize our problems, to bow down before the mountains and think this is acquiescence to the will of God. Christ came to demonstrate the art of mountain-*removing!*

And as we catch the echo of His voice, we sense an exuberant faith and a buoyant humor in Him that says to each of us; "So that's your problem? That isn't so bad! There's nothing here that My Father and I can't handle. Come, let us blast away this mountain!"

ACCEPT GOD'S GIFTS

For by grace you have been saved through faith,
and that not of yourselves; it is the gift of God. . . .

EPHESIANS 2:8

A woman whose poor health had been a severe drain on her family, was doing everything possible to be a devoted Christian. She felt God wanted her to establish a pattern of early morning Bible reading and prayer. Yet her conscience constantly bothered her because sometimes she managed the early hour and sometimes she didn't.

One day in desperation, she knelt by her bed. "Father," she prayed, "my poor health is ruining my family life. I'm not going to rise from my knees until You tell me where I'm failing."

Sometime during the next hour her eyes fell on the verse quoted above. With great emphasis God spoke to her mind, "You have been trying to earn healing with your morning hour. None of my good gifts can ever be earned. There's only one way to receive them—by grace, . . . by unmerited favor. Accept my gift now by faith."

PICKING PRIORITIES

Having been set free from sin,
and having become slaves of God,
you have your fruit to holiness.

ROMANS 6:22

*S*in is largely a matter of mistaken priorities. Any sin in us that is cherished, hidden, and not confessed will cut the nerve center of our faith. A guilty conscience will inevitably produce fear—the antithesis of faith.

For instance, resentment or lack of forgiveness will always be a stumbling block to faith (Mark 11:25). So will the wrong priorities of putting the world's approval ahead of God's approval (John 5:44). Yet every single one of us is a sinner. Then what shall we do with our sins? Be honest about them before God. Abandon them. Waste no time moaning about them. Accept forgiveness immediately—and our faith will flow back stronger than ever.

OUR SOURCE OF SUPPLY

It is better to trust in the LORD
than to put confidence in man.

PSALM 118:8

Of course, I believe that God can do anything," we are
fond of saying, "but. . . ." The "but" clearly reveals that
our faith does not go beyond intellectual belief. It leaves
our emotions and our wills—the twin springs of action—quite
untouched.

The truth is that most of us simply do not believe the Psalmist's
affirmation. We never rely on God alone until circumstances . . .
force us to do so.

Many Quakers on the American frontier threw away their
guns and trusted God for safety. . . . George Müeller, founder of
British orphanages, gave away his household goods, and refused
any regular salary to prove that God was his source of supply. . . .

How long has it been since we relied on God *alone* for anything—large or small—without trying in the meanwhile, to
work it out ourselves?

THE PAST IS GONE

The Lord is risen indeed!

LUKE 24:34

It does no good to look back and "suppose I had not answered the phone, or had taken the other turn in the road." The past is gone, and vital supposing can be done only in the living present. Even as Mary was searching for her Lord at the empty tomb and almost failed to recognize Him, so all of us become so engrossed in our grief and regret that we fail to see what could happen if we took a good look at what surrounds us now. When she looked again, she found the Christ. . . .

While other ideologies suppose there is no God, and that those who accept Him are weaklings, it remains for those who believe in Easter's risen Lord to suppose that His kingdom *can* come.

STRENGTH FROM SHARING

As each one has received a gift,
minister it to one another, as good stewards
of the manifold grace of God.

1 PETER 4:10

"Why should I go to church?" is a question often asked by the secularist. "I know folks inside the church. They're no better than I am. I just don't see the point. . . ."

Of course, church members aren't perfect. The church is a fellowship of sinners struggling to learn together the God-ordained secrets of happy living. One way for this strengthening of faith to happen is by sharing what we have learned of God through our own experiences. The man whom Jesus rescued from insanity wanted to follow Jesus to enjoy his fellowship. Instead, Jesus told him, "Go home to your friends, and tell them how much the Lord has done for you" (Mark 5:19).

How much of this kind of sharing are you making room for in your life?

WALKING THE FAITH ROAD

So if the Son makes you free, you will be free indeed.

JOHN 8:36

According to Jesus, it is God's will that His children have an unfettered self—a self filled with the joy of life.

This freeing of the self is the real purpose of righteousness: the rightness that God asks of His children. Yet all too often we have thought that righteousness means the end of all our fun and freedom. Nothing could be further from the truth. God's love means sheer goodwill for us. Each of us can find the truth for ourselves only as we, step by step, walk the Faith Road, for God sees to it that sight never precedes faith.

CHRIST THE CONQUEROR

Looking unto Jesus, the author and finisher of our faith. . . .

HEBREWS 12:2

E vil seems to rule our world. . . . Greed is rampant. As the contagious and infectious diseases are conquered, heart disease and cancer take an increasing toll. Evil seemed to rule the world even in Paul's day, yet he declared it a "dethroned power" (1 Cor. 2:6, MOFFATT).

How could he make that claim? Because of what happened on Easter morning. The message that rang throughout the Roman world and has never died out is that because Christ rose from the dead, sin, disease, and even the last enemy, death, have all been conquered.

Yet this victory is not ours until we claim it for ourselves by faith. Every day, as we walk by faith, is meant to be Easter Day!

SINGLE-MINDED SUCCESS

*That person must not suppose that
a double-minded man, unstable in all his ways,
will receive anything from the Lord.*

JAMES 1:7,8

A woman I know had been an invalid for quite a long time. Steadily, she had asked God to heal her. One day as she was praying, it seemed that Christ spoke deep in her heart, "Do you *really* want to get well?"

It seemed a ridiculous question. Yet, as she pondered it, her "double-minded" self was laid bare. With one part of her being she was actually enjoying the quiet life. She had time for reading and was free from all household duties. This revelation enabled her to pray with barefaced honesty, "Lord, I *am* divided. Will you now heal this breach and give me single-mindedness for health?"

The prayer was answered. For didn't Jesus promise that when any one of us become single-eyed our "whole body will be full of light?" (Matt. 6:22)

NEVER LOSE FAITH

Now don't be afraid, go on believing....
LUKE 8:50, PHILLIPS

*J*esus taught that answered prayer requires persistence. There may be a period when the door of blessing on which we hammer in prayer remains shut. Yet if we persist in knocking, the promise is that God will eventually open the door.

It helps to know that Jesus Himself warned us not to be surprised when we encounter this period of brass skies, ... the dark night of all-but-intolerable waiting, the piling up of obstacles. Why does God ask us to go through this? ... To help us develop faith muscles. Though we may not know "why," ... happy is the person who during this period of the closed door never loses faith in prayer.

ACCENTUATE THE POSITIVE

Apply your heart to instruction,
and your ears to words of knowledge.

PROVERBS 23:12

Our faith is built up and appropriated as we form habitual thought-patterns that accentuate the positive. Day after day our thoughts are either taking us toward life or toward death. There is no middle ground. Here is a check-list of negative thought characteristics:

criticism	(1 Cor. 4:5)
complaint	(Phil. 4:11)
condemnation	(Matt. 5:22)
resentment	(Mark 11:25)
fear	(Matt. 14:22)
worry	(Matt. 6:31)

Let us not think that we can habitually think in destructive ways and then—when a severe crisis comes in which we sorely need God's help—suddenly reverse these thought patterns and summon faith to help.

THE ESSENCE OF LOVE

*Love . . . bears all things, believes all things,
hopes all things, endures all things.*

1 CORINTHIANS 13:4,7

The gospels make it clear that to Jesus the Father is all-loving, is the essence of love, cannot help loving. Moreover, this love includes the attributes of love known to all of us—goodwill, unselfishness, consideration, justice, wanting only good things for us, desiring our happiness. It isn't a love dependent on our earning it. God is "for us" first, last, and always. By every word and action, by all the force of His personality, Christ sought to tell us that the Father is always nearer, mightier, freer to help us than we can imagine.

Some said that any man who held such ideas must be mad. But the disciples who tramped the dusty roads with Jesus day after day, who witnessed His decisiveness in dealing with people, His fearlessness of criticism, His sense of the sacredness of human personality, the realism with which He faced evil, knew that this One was not mad. Indeed, He was more beautifully sane than anyone they had ever known.

GETTING TO KNOW GOD

Faith comes by hearing,
and hearing by the word of God.

ROMANS 10:17

Why would Bible reading produce faith? Certainly not because there is something magical about the book. The real reasons are far more direct . . . : (1) We can scarcely claim God's promises for ourselves until we know what He has promised. (2) The Bible is a series of true stories of God's dealing with men and women quite like us.

There are pioneers, adventurers, and businessmen. There are the ever-present problems of greed, lust, and adultery. There is romance and drama. The Bible is never less than frank; it never whitewashes sin. When we read this book intelligently, we learn how God deals with humankind, what He is like, and what we can expect from Him.

GIVING UP SELF WILL

Until now you have asked nothing in My name.
Ask, and you will receive, that your joy may be full.

JOHN 16:24

From my sick bed of many months I prayed. "I'm tired of asking. I'm beaten, finished. God, You decide what you want for me for the rest of my life." Tears flowed. I had no faith as I understood faith. I expected nothing. Turning the gift of my sick self over to God was done with no trace of graciousness.

Yet the result was as if windows had opened in heaven; as if some dynamo of heavenly power had begun flowing into me. From that moment my recovery began. . . .

God was trying to teach me something important about prayer. . . . I saw that the demanding spirit—"God, I must have thus and so; God, this is what I want you to do for me—" is not real prayer and hence receives no answer. The reason for this is that God absolutely refuses to violate our free will; therefore, unless self-will is voluntarily given up, even God cannot move to answer our prayer.

THE GIFT OF FAITH

There are diversities of gifts, but the same Spirit . . .
given to each one for the profit of all.

1 CORINTHIANS 12:4,7

A very sincere and thoughtful Christian knows he can no more get along without faith than a fish can survive out of water. But the question is how does one get this faith . . . this ability to trust God actively whom our five senses cannot perceive?

Have you ever asked God for the gift of faith? Or is this so obvious you've overlooked it? Be sure, however, that you really want what you ask for. Praying can be "dangerous business." If you ask for piano lessons, you'll have to do some practicing. If you ask for faith, you'll probably encounter situations immediately that will call for complete trust in God alone.

May

The scope of God's blessing is much wider
and deeper and higher than most of us know.

THE PERFECT PATTERN FOR PRAYER

I, even I, am the LORD, and besides Me there is no Savior.

ISAIAH 43:11

To the disciples of Jesus Christ, His actions during the last week of His life on earth must have seemed . . . nonsensical. Their Master had a great following among the common people. His disciples were hoping that He would use this following to overthrow the Roman grip on their little country and move, at last, to establish His earthly kingdom.

Instead, He deliberately set His feet on the path that would lead inescapably to the cross. For let us not mistake it. Christ could have avoided that cross. . . . Even in the Garden of Gethsemane on the night of betrayal, Christ had plenty of time and opportunity to flee.

But He would not flee. Instead, He knelt to pray in the shadowy Garden under the gray-green leaves of the olive tress. And in His prayer that night, Jesus gave us, for all time, the perfect pattern for the Prayer of Relinquishment: "Not what I want, but what You want." . . . Jesus deliberately set Himself to make His will and God's will the same.

FORGIVENESS FROM THE HEART

If you forgive men their trespasses,
your heavenly Father will also forgive you.

MATTHEW 6:14

At the heart of the gospel lies forgiveness, the greatest miracle of all. Only as we open ourselves to receive this most wondrous of gifts, can the inner self deep within us be freed to become the happier, finer persons we are meant to be. . . .

Yet forgiveness has two sides that are inseparably joined: the forgiveness each of us needs from God, and the forgiveness we owe to other human beings. Most of us prefer not to face up to the fact that God's forgiveness and man's are forever linked.

But Jesus warned us that if we want the Father's forgiveness, there is only one way to get it: Start the flow of forgiveness between heaven and earth by forgiving others from the heart.

PRACTICE OBEDIENCE

Your word is a lamp to my feet and a light to my path.

PSALM 119:105

Here are some truths about guidance, a few time-tested suggestions, I have found useful:

Obey one step at a time, then the next step will come into view. God will not give us a blueprint of the future; He still insists that our walk be step by step in faith.

As we practice obedience, His inner guidance becomes clearer, His instructions more definite. Perhaps it should not surprise us that with guidance, as with anything else, we learn through practice.

That is why it is wise to give God a chance to speak to us each day, perhaps the first thing in the morning when the mind is freshest. A few minutes of quietness helps us focus on the areas where we most need God's help.

LINKED TO GOD'S POWER

By You I can run against a troop,
by my God I can leap over a wall.

PSALM 18:29

was able to write *A Man Called Peter* only after I learned to see my human helplessness in the endeavor as the crucible out of which victory could rise. I learned that although I was inadequate, God was adequate. He knew the secret of successful creative effort. I did not. . . . I learned that when achievement has come because of our helplessness linked to God's power, it has a rightness about it that no amount of self-inspired striving can have. Furthermore, when achievement comes this way, it does not bear in it the seeds of increasing egocentricity that success sometimes brings. Because we know that ideas and the ability to implement them flowed into us from somewhere beyond ourselves, we can be objective about our good fortune.

THE JOY OF FULLFILLMENT

You yourselves are taught
by God to love on another.
1 THESSALONIANS 4:9

*I*t is not surprising that thinking first of the other person is the first step to love. But one cannot feign interest in other people; when it is artificial, it fools nobody. In this day of psychiatric know-how, we are aware that acute self-centeredness is a sign of mental illness and that giving up egocentricity is necessary for the integration of character.

But how does one achieve this? Surely not by saying, "From this moment, I will be unselfish and outgoing." Personally, I have found no sure way to faith except that simple formula of handing one's will and one's self over to God. He alone can shift the gears in us from dullness to warmth, from preoccupation with self to a lively interest in others, from that "toothache of the spirit" to the joy of fulfillment.

PATIENCE AND TRUST

Wait on the LORD; be of good courage,
and He shall strengthen your heart; wait, I say, on the LORD!

PSALM 27:14, MOFFATT

A friend of mine desperately wanted a certain job. She believed that the job was God's will for her. She had frequently prayed about it, yet nothing seemed to happen. In her mind was the haunting question, "How much should I do about this and how much should I leave to God?"

Do we really believe that we can ask God a direct question and get a direct answer? If so, then let us ask God what to do in order to show Him our faith—then do only that. Any other activity on our part, especially any action that springs out of impatience or lack of trust in Him—(and honesty is needed here)—is wrong.

Often it seems to us that God moves slowly; that He refuses to accept the mad pace of our century. "*Stand still* and see the salvation of the Lord . . . " Moses ordered the children of Israel (Exod. 14:13). Ah! But standing still requires patience and trust!

CHARACTERISTICS OF CHRIST

I am the good shepherd.
The good shepherd gives His life for the sheep.

JOHN 10:11

was going through the Gospels consecutively to get a vivid portrait of Jesus. And a portrait did emerge. Not so much what He looked like, as the characteristics of His person. I discovered in Him one who is totally alive—physically stalwart, emotionally sensitive. Humor, I definitely found. And grief—not for Himself, but for others' hurts and the tragic havoc that sin brings. And love, an amazing love that pours out of Him with never any effort to hide it or dam it up. Yet it is a love with steel in it.

Over and over I have come upon this steel—a note of stringency in Jesus' conversation and His way of dealing with people. . . . Never have I found a trace of coddling or compromising or self-protectiveness in Him.

A DEFINITE DECISION

You must not let yourselves be distressed.
You must hold on to your faith in God and to your faith in Me.

JOHN 14:1, PHILLIPS

*E*ach of us already possesses a deposit of faith as God's gift. But do we handle this initial faith so that it grows or do we let it slip away? "That is up to *you*," Jesus told us. "The secret resides in the human will."

There comes a point in the matter of trusting God for a real need, when to continue to rely on Him alone seems terribly risky. A definite decision involving our wills then has to be made. Will we decide to stake everything on God, or will we turn back and try human resources? Scripture tells us that what we *do* is the important thing—not how we *feel*; that only as we proceed to act out our trust, will the emotion of confident faith well up within us.

GOOD AND PERFECT GIFTS

Every good gift and every perfect gift is from above.

JAMES 1:17

Everything God asks us to do is for our good—not just our spiritual welfare—but good as you and I understand it.

A girl was deeply in love, engaged to a boy whose standards did not seem high enough. She became convinced that God wanted her to break the engagement. In this case, it looked as if God's glory sharply conflicted with her happiness. But with a rare depth of consecration, the girl made the great sacrifice.

A year later she met the man whose life perfectly supplemented her own. She knew then that her perfect happiness had been God's plan all along.

The truth is that when we make God's will our will, our deepest happiness and welfare also glorifies Him and extends His kingdom on earth. We can trust a God like that!

ACCEPTANCE OR RESIGNATION?

This is the victory that has overcome the world—our faith.

1 JOHN 5:4

There is a difference between acceptance and resignation. One is positive; the other negative. . . .

Resignation is barren of faith in the love of God. It says, "Grievous circumstances have come to me. There is no escaping them. . . . I have no heart left even to rebel. So I'll just resign myself to what apparently is the will of God; . . ." So resignation lies down quietly in the dust of a universe from which God seems to have fled, and the door of hope swings shut.

But turn the coin over. Acceptance says, "I trust the goodwill, the love of my God. I'll open my arms and my understanding to what He has allowed to come to me. Since I know that He means to make all things work together for good, I consent to this present situation with hope for what the future will bring." Thus acceptance leaves the door of hope wide open to God's creative plan.

FORGIVE FREELY

If indeed I have forgiven anything,
I have forgiven that one for your sakes
in the presence of Christ.

2 CORINTHIANS 2:10

esus had a great deal to say about forgiveness. Take the scene recorded by Matthew . . . : The disciples know that according to old Jewish law, one must forgive three times. After that, a man can be as hostile to another as he wishes.

But impetuous Peter is feeling expansive. He draws his striped robe about him and asks, "Lord, how oft shall my brother sin against me and I forgive him?" A smug look creeps across the disciple's face. He will be overly generous in answering his own question and so win a word of approval from the Master; "Until seven times?"

Christ looks at His disciple, His eyes showing amusement. Peter is so transparent, always ready to talk. "Your arithmetic is all wrong, Simon, as wrong as that of the scribes and Pharisees. Forgive seven times? Nay—seventy times seven."

THE SWEET MUSIC OF FAITH

Faith comes by hearing,
and hearing by the word of God.

JOHN 10:17

Once I thought that faith was believing this or that specific thing in my mind with never a doubt. Now I know that faith is nothing more or less than actively trusting God. . . .

We demonstrate trust by placing the thing or person or situation we are concerned about into the Father's hands to do with as He pleases. . . . This is faith in action.

This relinquishment brings answers to prayers, even when we have little hope that what we fear most can be avoided. For . . . God is not half so concerned about our having a few negative thoughts as He is concerned with what we do. And the act of placing what we cherish most in His hands is to Him the sweet music of the essence of faith.

FORGIVE ONE ANOTHER

Forgive us our debts, as we forgive our debtors.

MATTHEW 6:12

Our debt to the Heavenly Father is inordinate, unpayable. We are at the mercy of His compassion. In comparison with our debt to Him, the most any human being can owe us is trifling.

Every one of us is guilty before God. There are sins of the mind and the spirit as well as of the body. There are unworthy motives. There are all the opportunities that have gone begging away. There are all the times we have chosen second best. Yet God is willing freely to forgive us, no matter what we have done, provided we are willing to be "kind one to another, tenderhearted, forgiving one another, even as God in Christ forgave you" (Eph. 4:32).

DIRECT GUIDANCE

In all your ways acknowledge Him,
and He shall direct your paths.

PROVERBS 3:6

f decisions—large and small—can be so important, on what basis shall we make them? Without
God, most of us muddle through somehow, often with
better hindsight than foresight. . . .

Christianity from the first has taught that a better way for
making decisions is available: the direct guidance of God to the
individual. The promise that God can guide us is the clear teaching
of Scripture, both in its total sweep and in its specific promises.

This Scriptural teaching rests on three pillars: (1) that God
has all wisdom, hence knows the past and the future and what
is best for His children; (2) that He is a God of love who cares
about us as individuals enough to want to direct us right; (3) that
He can communicate with us. As Abraham Lincoln once
commented, "I am satisfied that when the Almighty wants me
to do, or not to do any particular thing, He finds a way of
letting me know it."

NATURAL SELF OR NEW SELF?

Whoever desires to come after Me,
let him deny himself, and take up his cross, and follow Me.

MARK 8:34

Each of us is tinctured with self-will; with self-ambitions; with the desire to be pampered, cushioned, and admired; with over-criticalness of everyone else and over-sensitiveness about ourselves; with a drive to enlarge the self with an accumulation of things. Thus, try as we may to separate these self-centered qualities from the unselfish ones, the self keeps cropping up again and again, tripping us every time.

What is Christ's solution to our dilemma? It is recorded for us in the eighth chapter of Mark. "Whoever desires to save his life will lose it," he says, "but whoever loses his life for My sake . . . shall save it" (Mark 8:35). To put it another way, there is no solution apart from the painful . . . handing over to Him all of our natural self to be destroyed so that He can give us a new self—one born from above, one in which He will live at the center of our being.

PRECIOUS PROMISES

Imitate those who through faith
and patience inherit the promises.
HEBREWS 6:12

friend of mine was facing surgery, filled with fear. She knew this fear would make her a poor surgical risk. "Lord, how can I get rid of this?" she prayed. "I've tried, but I can't handle it." During the next few minutes, words from Hebrews 13:5 came clearly to her mind: "I will never fail you nor forsake you."

"This is Your Word, Lord," she prayed. "I claim it as a promise for myself right now. I know that where You are, there can be no fear." Her prayer was answered almost immediately. The fear left, and she sailed through surgery successfully.

Have you discovered this prayer technique of claiming in faith the specific promise the Holy Spirit impresses upon your mind for any given need? Try it for yourself!

LET GOD DO THE WORK

He who will not believe God, has made God a liar. . . .

1 JOHN 5:10, MOFFATT

The strengthening of faith comes through staying with it in the hour of trial. We should not shrink from tests of our faith. Only when we are depending on God alone are we in a position to see God's help and deliverance, and thus have our faith strengthened.

This means that we must let Him do the work. Almost always it takes longer than we think it should. When we grow impatient and try a deliverance of our own, through friends or circumstances, we are taking God's work out of His hands. . . .

The adventure of living has not really begun until we begin to stand on our faith legs and claim—for ourselves, for our homes, for the rearing of our children, for our health problems, for our business affairs, and for our world—the resources of our God.

OUR ABSURDITIES

*Whoever humbles himself as this little child
is the greatest in the kingdom of heaven.*

MATTHEW 18:4

Once we reread the Gospels, watching for Christ's wit, we find it everywhere. "Can one blind man be guide to another blind man? Surely they will both fall into the ditch together" (Matt. 15:14).

Thus if we will read them carefully, the Gospels give us a picture of a Christ who would not let people be unobservant about life, about the actions of others, or most of all, about themselves. He wanted them awakened at every level of their being. And so He used every weapon of language and thought and communication to achieve His goals. Most effective were banter, the humorous thrust and sardonic comments about those who put on airs and think more highly of themselves than they should. As one of sound and balanced mind, He could not observe humankind and fail to see our incongruities and absurdities. He does see, and He laughs along with us.

BEYOND FORGIVENESS

Love is the fulfillment of the law.

ROMANS 13:10

s I look out over the bright greenery of our backyard this morning, I realize how hard it is for me to love people, even members of my own family, when I disapprove of their behavior. I know this is wrong, Lord Jesus, because You demonstrated time after time that it is possible, even necessary, to love people without judgment.

There was the woman taken in adultery and about to be stoned when You asked the mob surrounding her, "If any one of you is without sin, let him be the first to throw a stone at her." As You told her to go and sin no more, I could almost hear the caring quality of Your voice. Likewise the woman You met at the well, the one who had had five husbands. Uncondemning love was in Your manner.

I have no trouble forgiving certain people, but recently I have seen that the forgiveness is not complete in Your eyes until I can love them too.

GOD CLEARS THE WAY

Whoever loves instruction loves knowledge.

PROVERBS 12:1

When we have asked God to guide us, we have to accept by faith the fact that He is doing so. This means that when He closes a door in our faces, then we do well not to try to crash that door.

Sensitivity is needed here. When God is guiding us, we need not ride roughshod over other people's viewpoints, lives, and affairs. The promise is that the Shepherd will go ahead of the sheep; His method is to clear the way for us. . . .

It is true that sometimes God asks us to do something . . . we cannot understand at the time. But He does not ask us to cancel out the minds or ignore the common sense He has given us, except in most unusual circumstances.

SEVEN SPIRITUAL STEPS

If these things are yours and abound,
you will be neither barren nor unfruitful in the
knowledge of our Lord Jesus Christ.

2 PETER 1:8

In Second Peter chapter one, the apostle rejoices in the "precious and very great promises" by which we may be "partakers of the divine nature." Then he gives us a ladder of seven steps leading to this high goal:

1. To faith, add *virtue.* (v. 5)

2. To virtue, add *knowledge.* (v. 5)

3. To knowledge, add *self-control.* (v. 6)

4. To self-control, add *steadfastness.* (v. 6)

5. To steadfastness, add *godliness.* (v. 6)

6. To godliness, add *brotherly affection.* (v. 7)

7. To brotherly affection will then be added, *love.* (v. 7)

I want to climb that ladder, Lord, to be able to know You and love You more than ever before.

THE HEIGHTS OF LIFE

He makes my feet like hinds' feet,
and sets me upon my high places.

PSALM 18:33, NASB

Auntie Chamberlain—a woman who gave herself totally to life—taught me the importance of doing every task with my whole heart.

Piano lessons took on added luster when I not only learned to read a piece of music, but also memorized it. School assignments were more fun when I did more than the minimum required. And I found that something more important than good grades came from this approach—a deep inner satisfaction, a glow, a happiness. . . .

It's the secret of hinds' feet. The rear feet of the female red deer, known also as the *hind,* step in precisely the same spot where the front feet have just been. Every motion of the hind is followed through with this same single-focused consistency, making it the most sure-footed of all mountain animals.

As the feet of the female deer are to the mountains, so is the mind of man to the heights of life.

THE ETERNAL NOW

Which is easier to say,
"Your sins are forgiven you," or to say,
"Rise up and walk"?

LUKE 5:23

A man had great problems. He had heard of Jesus of Nazareth. Was there just a chance that the Master might be able to help *him?* But this man was ill, unable even to walk, paralyzed. In the end, four of his solicitous friends carried the sick man on a stretcher to see Jesus.

Christ straightened out that man's present and future by straightening out his past. Thus God always works, for with Him there are no time compartments, only the eternal *now.* Our past sins—if not forgiven—are still in the present tense, still a part of us.

Do you have any problems in the present? The way to solve them is to let Jesus deal with your past. Then your present and future will fall into place as surely as the sun will rise tomorrow.

NO PRETENSE OR HYPOCRISY

The works of the LORD are great,
studied by all who have pleasure in them.

PSALM 111:2

here is an unexpected dividend from reading the New Testament as if Jesus were speaking to me. When I look away from the problems in my new marriage to turn my full attention to Jesus, He proves Himself alive by concerning Himself with my life, family, and friends and talking to me about these matters morning after morning.

Last week, for example, as I read the twelfth chapter of Luke, it was as though Jesus were saying: Beware of pretending before the family to be something you are not, or to have attained spiritual values that you have not attained. This is hypocrisy. And nothing is more futile than trying to keep anything secret. There is nothing covered up among family members that is not going to be uncovered.

WAS JESUS RIGHT?

So they went out and preached that
men should change their whole outlook.

MARK 6:13, PHILLIPS

Those who knew Jesus found in Him something altogether new in their experience. What was so extraordinary about Jesus' beliefs that His Father is all love and has nothing but goodwill for us, His children;

* that God has all power and all limits to that power are on our part, not God's;
* that God has complete freedom to answer prayer in every area of life;
* that we win the Father's response only by faith through prayer?

For a time, the impact of the personality of the God-man and the stupendous deeds that the apostles saw so convinced them that they, too, performed the deeds that Christ did. But in the centuries since, something has happened to chill our ideas about God.

Was Jesus right? Or was He somehow deluded?

GOD IS ALWAYS ADEQUATE

Those who know Your name will put their trust in You;
for You, LORD, have not forsaken those who seek You.

PSALM 9:10

he tragedies most difficult to take are those that come through the failures, ignorance, carelessness, or hatred of other human beings. There are times when men seem to be working havoc with God's plans. I had a friend, for instance, . . . who died because of an error made by a pharmacist in filling a prescription. . . .

It is important that we believe that God is adequate even for these situations. . . . In order to fly, the bird must have two wings. One wing is the realization of our human helplessness, the other is the realization of God's power. Our faith in God's ability to handle our particular situation is the connecting link. . . .

If we cannot believe that God can help us recover from troubles shaped by human beings as well as those we bring upon ourselves, then we have a narrow basis indeed for our faith in Him.

A PLAN FOR PROTECTION

They shall be My people, and I will be their God.

JEREMIAH 24:7

God loved the children He created. He longed to save them from costly blunders. Being God, He possessed the wisdom they needed. But how could He get them to accept this wisdom?

God evolved a plan. He would start with one obedient man, Abraham. From Abraham would spring a whole race—the Jewish nation. God would show this nation how to live, what laws to make, so they might be happy. They would become God's blueprint on this planet.

The Old Testament is the unfolding story of this Plan. Its success was dependent on man's obedience. Much of it had to be blind obedience, for how could a primitive nomad people understand the reason for things like sanitation, quarantine and soil conservation?

The Israelites thought of God's detailed laws as mere ceremonial worship. We know those laws were made for their protection and happiness.

SPIRITUAL STARVATION

He knelt down on his knees three times that day,
and prayed and gave thanks before his God,
as was his custom since early days.

DANIEL 6:10

t was Carol, my friend from California, who made me aware that spiritual undernourishment can be quite as real as physical starvation. . . . She felt tired all the time from the daily routine. "Nothing is much fun anymore," she had said. "I have so little energy that no undertaking seems worth attempting. What's wrong with me?"

An hour and much talk later, I had a sudden inspiration: could it be that Carol's inner spirit was starving to death?

"We have three meals a day," I suggested to her. "Perhaps we need spiritual food three times a day too."

"But what *is* spiritual food? And how do you take it?" she asked.

I replied. "Jesus said that His words are spirit and life indeed. . . . He described himself as 'living water' and 'the bread of life'. Meeting Him in Scripture is like an intravenous feeding from His Spirit to our spirit."

FAITH IN WHAT?

*Now faith means we are confident
of what we hope for, convinced of what we do not see.*

HEBREWS 11:1, MOFFATT

aith is believing something specific in the present and acting on that belief. The deeds that follow our prayers are the telltale signs of whether or not faith is actually present.

Everyone has faith. The important question is: faith in what or in *whom*? In natural law? In science? In the government? In the power of evil? In one's own powers? Or in God?

Each of us believes *something*. But do we believe a lie? Or do we believe God's truth? New Testament faith always assumes (never argues) a loving, articulate God's personal dealings with individuals. Therefore, living by faith means we believe God when He tells us that He either has given us a particular blessing or will bestow it. Then we act out our trust, expecting Him to keep His word.

THE CREATOR STILL CREATES

I chose you . . . that you should go and bear fruit.

JOHN 15:16

*J*esus is God in action. His every teaching insists on the positive, the creative.

He did not come to judge the world, but to save it (John 12:47); He wants His disciples to have joy—that most positive of all emotions (John 15:11).

Jesus never subtracts. He always adds or multiplies. He came not to destroy or subtract one iota of the Law, but to fulfill it (Matt.5:17). He praised the two faithful servants who multiplied their talents, condemned the one who merely hung on to the status quo (Matt. 25:14–30). He multiplied the [loaves] and fishes, so there was a twelve-basket surplus (Matt. 14:16–21). . . .

He insists that each of us be a fruit-bearing Christian . . . (John 15:2). The Kingdom of God is positive creativity.

A TRIANGLE OF AUTHORITY

Wives, submit to your own husbands as to the Lord.

EPHESIANS 5:22

The hub upon which the Ephesian "submission" passages turn is the statement that introduces them: "Be subject to one another out of reverence for Christ" (Eph. 5:21, AMP). This is the irreducible minimum of Paul's instructions to all Christians—male or female.

This is a triangle of authority more than a pecking order. God is at the apex of the triangle; the husband and wife are equally positioned at the lower corners. Thus both mates are equal in His sight, equally beloved by Him, equally committed to each other and to Him.

Len and I are finding "Be subject to one another out of reverence for Christ" to be intensely practical. It means a spirit of mutual respect, a willingness to listen. It means giving—and sometimes giving in—on the part of both of us, since sometimes God gives His direction to me through my husband.

June

Our prayers must not be efforts to bend
God to our will but to yield ourselves to His.

THE PURSUIT OF HAPPINESS

Whoever desires to save his life will lose it,
but whoever loses his life for My sake will find it.

MATTHEW 16:25

A believe the secret of happiness lies imbedded in those words, painful though they appear to be. I have observed that when any of us embarks on the pursuit of happiness for ourselves, it eludes us. Often I've asked myself why. It must be because happiness comes to us only as a dividend. When we become absorbed in something demanding and worthwhile above and beyond ourselves, happiness seems to be there as a by-product of the self-giving.

That should not be a startling truth, yet I'm surprised at how few people understand and accept it. Have we made a god of happiness? Have we been brainwashed by ads assuring us "Happiness is . . ."—usually a big, shiny, new gadget?

NO NEED IS TOO TRIVIAL

He will not allow your foot to be moved;
He who keeps you will not slumber.

PSALM 121:3

After the Bible study I gave last week on praying for all our needs, no matter how small, one woman took sharp issue with me: "Asking for small things is being selfish," she remonstrated.

I could only reply that this was not Jesus' viewpoint as presented in the Gospels. Both by teaching and by action He impressed upon us that no need is too trivial for His attention.

I've combed Scripture for examples and there are many, such as: The wine needed at a wedding feast (John 2:1–11); a dying sparrow (Matt. 10:29); a lost lamb (Luke 15:3-7).

These vignettes, scattered through the Gospels like little patches of gold dust, say to us, "No earthly need is outside the scope of prayer."

LOOK TO GOD'S PROMISE

Your mercy, O LORD, endures forever;
do not forsake the works of Your hands.

PSALM 138:8

he Holy Spirit showed me that I had fallen hook, line, and sinker for one of Satan's oldest and most-used tricks: looking steadily at the difficulty instead of at Jesus. . . . He further reminded me that my husband, children, and grandchildren are not mine, but God's. He's not only as concerned as I am for them, but loves them far more than I ever could. Therefore, I must take my possessive, self-centered hands off—strictly off. So, in an act of relinquishment, I did this. . . .

Suddenly these words leapt from the page: "The LORD will perfect that which concerns me . . . forsake not the works of Your own hands" (Psalm 138:8, AMP).

I could—and did—claim this promise promptly for my family. Years ago the Lord began a work in these lives. It's His business to perfect what He started. He has promised that He will. I've claimed and accepted that promise. It's as good as done.

GOD'S WILL BE DONE

And all flesh shall see the salvation of God.

LUKE 3:6

In giving mankind free will, God has given us a long rope. When we see the suffering godless men can bring on our world, we sometimes wish the rope were not quite as long. But we need to remember that the Father has not abdicated. God still holds the end of the rope.

There are definite limits to the evil God allows men to perpetrate. Evil is self-defeating and self-destructive. This is the encouraging lesson that history would teach us.

It is true that God's purposes can be temporarily frustrated. His plans can suffer setbacks in time. But, in the end, His purposes cannot be defeated. God's will, will be done in us and "on earth as it is in heaven."

A STUNNING THOUGHT

The Son of man came not to be waited on but to serve.

MATTHEW 20:28, AMP

When Jesus wrapped a towel around his waist, poured water into a basin, and began to wash His disciples' feet (see John 13:4–5), Simon Peter objected that this was beneath the dignity of the Master. *We* the disciples are to be the servants, I want to insist along with Peter. But Jesus answered him, "If I do not wash you, you have no part in me."

This is a stunning and stupendous thought. Unless I can believe in *this much* love for me, unless I can and will accept Him with faith as my servant as well as my God, unless I truly know that it's *my* good He seeks, not His glory (He already has all of that He can use for all eternity), *then I cannot have His companionship.*

THE THRONE OF OUR HEARTS

Our old man was crucified with Him,
that the body of sin might be done away with,
that we should no longer be slaves of sin.

ROMANS 6:6

To the Apostle Paul the matter of handing over the whole self to Christ . . . was at the heart of Christianity. "For we know that our old self was crucified with Him (that is, with Christ) to do away with our sin-loving body, so that we might not be enslaved to sin any longer."

To Paul the essence of sin lay in a person's life being ruled by "my will be done" rather than by "God's will be done." There is, he was saying, a fundamental choice at the heart of life. It is simply "Who is going to be the master?" And if we fail to make a conscious choice in this, then we make it by default. In that case, self will rule from the throne of our hearts.

GOD IN HUMAN FORM

*Believe the works [I do], that you may know
and believe that the Father is in Me, and I in Him.*

JOHN 10:37

esus claimed for Himself the prerogative of God: He claimed the right to forgive and to wipe out sins (Luke 5:20–24) .

He claimed authority over all natural forces (Mark 4:37–41; Luke 5:5–6).

He claimed authority over the Law of Supply (Mark 10:51–52; Luke 7:20–23).

He claimed authority over the last and final enemy—death (John 8:51).

If Jesus of Nazareth were God in human form, are not these exactly the claims we would *expect* Him to make? And if these claims are true, then this is the most exciting discovery any human being can make.

TURN CRITICISM TO PRAYER

Let us not judge one another anymore.

ROMANS 14:13

am determined to dig in on the matter of my critical nature. I do not like it. It's negative; yes, often destructive. Jesus warned us not to be judgmental. So did Paul. I have tried to excuse myself by saying that one must evaluate situations and people. It won't wash. It still comes out judging, a haughty superiority, which is the opposite of love.

How do we sensitive, critical people deal with our condition? I had one very direct answer from the Lord recently after I had loosed a blast of angry criticism at one of our national leaders at the luncheon table. God said to me, "Do not criticize at all" (1 Cor. 4:5 MOFFATT). "You spread negativism around you and pollute your own atmosphere when you do so. Turn your criticism and your indignation to good use by praying for that leader right now."

A good handle for me to grasp!

COMMISSIONED BY CHRIST

As the Father has sent Me, I also send you.

JOHN 20:21

Everywhere Jesus went great crowds gathered. The need was so great and there was so little time.

One of the few specific things Jesus ever asked us to pray for was people to act as representatives in His ministry of love—laborers to help gather the harvest (Matt. 9:37–38). . . . The gospels make it quite clear that in Jesus' mind His miracles were not unique with Him and were never meant to be confined to His lifetime on earth.

And so He sent out the twelve apostles to teach, to preach, and to heal (Matt. 10:5–8). Then He sent out thirty-five pairs of workers to preach the kingdom and heal the sick (Luke 10:9). After the Resurrection, He commissioned the larger group of disciples. . . . And lastly Jesus commissioned us (Matt. 28:19).

LET CHRIST CARRY THE LOAD

You will keep him in perfect peace,
whose mind is stayed on You, because he trusts in you.

ISAIAH 26:3

esterday I began trying to get back to a real *quiet time* in the early morning. My directive was, "Never mind about reading. Spend the time getting in touch with Jesus directly."

For a couple of days prior to this the Holy Spirit had dropped a curious clause from Scripture into my mind and heart: "And the government will be upon [Jesus'] shoulder . . ." (Isa. 9:6). I had never thought of this in relation to the government of *my* life. Suddenly it spoke volumes to me . . . the responsibility of my life is now His, the burden *He* will carry. He will make the decisions, the right decisions. What a relief: what joy to turn it over to Him.

Yesterday I mostly just asked Him questions, knowing that sooner or later in His time, He will answer them. He well knows my questioning spirit and I don't think He minds. . . . Having posed my questions, I left them there, in His hands . . . and felt sweet peace flowed into my spirit.

GOD IS OUR GUIDE

If any of you lacks wisdom, let him ask God . . .
in faith with no doubting.

JAMES 1:6–7

A mother was anxious to find the right school for her son. So she wrote for school catalogs, visited campuses, and made inquiries of many friends. "How," she wondered, "out of this welter of possibilities, can I find just the right school for my son?"

Finally, she prayed about this very practical problem. "Lord, a wisdom beyond my own is needed here." Then she proceeded to claim the Apostle James' wonderful promise for wisdom. Soon a chain of events was set in motion involving two strangers and a long-absent friend. The mother and son were led directly to a school not even previously considered.

The boy's first letter home closed with the words, "Mom, we really found the right school for me. I'm enjoying every minute of it!"

RIGHT ON THE INSIDE

I do not set aside the grace of God;
for if righteousness comes through the law,
then Christ died in vain.

GALATIANS 2:21

Many of us have entered the Christian life by faith. But having entered, we are inclined to shift our ground. We come to feel that we will become righteous (that is, remain acceptable to God) only as we *do* certain things.

Yet with a concerted voice, the New Testament writers teach that God's supreme interest is in what we *are*, not what we *do*. . . . One can do all the right moral things and still have a rotten heart. Conversely, if the heart is right then good deeds will inevitably follow.

But how do we get right on the inside? The New Testament supplies the secret: Abraham was not counted "good" by God because of what he did. Rather, "Abraham believed God and it was accounted to him for righteousness" (Rom. 4:3).

THE MISSING KEY

If anyone loves Me, he will keep My word; and My Father will love him.

JOHN 14:23

I was struggling this morning with the seeming contradiction between Jesus' constant stress on *obedience* as crucial to Christian growth, over against the reality of *grace*, which is the "unmerited favor of God."

I'm beginning to see that the missing key here is love. The chief characteristic of love is wanting to do what pleases the beloved. The analogy Jesus used most often was filial love: He meant His relationship to His Father to be the pattern for *our* relationship to Him (Jesus). Jesus' obedience was not the result of gritted teeth and grim determination, but the natural outworking of love: "I do as the Father has commanded me, so that the world may know (be convinced) that I love the Father . . ." (John 14:31, AMP).

MINISTERING TO JESUS

*My little children, let us not love
in word or in tongue, but in deed and in truth.*

1 JOHN 3:18

hen we truly love someone, our focus is on *him* or *her,* not on ourselves. And our constant thought is, "What can I do to give this beloved person joy? To please him? To ease his path? To minister to him?"

It staggers my mind to think that I can in any way minister to Jesus, or gladden His heart. Yet this is the gracious message of the gospel, which always puts the emphasis on love: "We love Him, because He first loved us" (1 John 4:19).

PRAY ABOUT EVERYTHING

Be anxious for nothing, but in everything
by prayer and supplication, with thanksgiving,
let your requests be made known to God.

PHILIPPIANS 4:6

he Apostle Paul exhorts us to pray about *everything,* to pour our hearts out to the Heavenly Father with "definite requests."

My problem is that having done this, having laid my concern before the Father, I get the feeling that if I do not frequently return to it in my mind and keep "worrying" it, much as a dog would a bone, then there certainly can be no chance of solving it. It's a feeling that it would actually be irresponsible or frivolous *not* to do this—wrong to think about other things, and go my merry way while a major problem sits before me.

I slip into the worry stance in spite of telling myself over and over that God is the problem-solver, that we can confidently leave our situation in His hands. I know what I should do, yet emotionally and practically I do not act out this letting go.

TOTAL TRUST

It is God who works in you both to
will and to do for His good pleasure.

PHILIPPIANS 2:13

An American soldier found a shy, terror-stricken . . . orphan hiding near his barracks. In the child's eyes was the look of a hurt animal. Later the G. I. commented, "In trying to help that little fellow, for the first time I really understood why God asks faith of His creatures. In the end there was only one way for that fear-filled child to know that my intentions for him were all good. He had to trust himself to me blindly."

Even so, the gap of understanding between finite man and infinite God is far wider than the chasm between the American soldier and the . . . war orphan. There is but one way to span that gap. That is to throw out the bridge of faith, then trust one's weight on the bridge and start across.

God does not require faith of us as a sort of coin or passport to heaven's treasures. Faith is for *our* benefit. It's the bridge to the blessings of God.

REJOICE IN THE LORD

Rejoice in the Lord always.
Again I will say, rejoice!

PHILIPPIANS 4:4

Regardless of any circumstances, we are to rejoice in the Lord always.

We are *not* to fret or to have anxiety about *anything*.

We are to pray about everything, making our needs and wants known unto God.

We are to be content with our earthly lot, whatever it is.

We are to guard our thoughts, thinking only upbeat, positive things—nothing negative.

If we will do these things, we are promised:

A. God's peace . . . shall garrison and mount guard over our hearts and minds in Christ Jesus.

B. Christ will "infuse inner strength into us"—that is, "We will be self-sufficient in Christ's sufficiency."

PEACE AND REST

There remains . . . a rest for the people of God.
For he who has entered into His rest
has himself also ceased from his works.

HEBREWS 4:9-10

In the midst of disquiet about so many things in our life right now—my trying to make progress on my novel—the message Jesus wants me to have today seems to be simply, "Peace! Rest in Me. I'm here to give you, Catherine, the precious gift of peace of mind and spirit."

How glorious! He confirms it in Scripture after Scripture: "May grace (God's favor) and *peace* (which is perfect well-being, all necessary good, all spiritual prosperity and freedom from fears and agitating passions and moral conflicts), be multiplied to you in the knowledge of God and of Jesus our Lord" (2 Pet. 1:2).

OBEDIENCE DAY BY DAY

Why do you call me Lord, Lord,
and not do the things which I say?

LUKE 6:46

Over the years I found that the evangelist of my childhood, Gypsy Smith, had been right in insisting that the only way we can really know God is by looking at Jesus Christ. Christ is the center of Christianity. To pretend anything else—that we need think of Him only as a good man who was also a great teacher, for instance—is not Christianity, whatever else it may be.

But I was also astonished to discover that no mere intellectual acceptance of Christ's divinity would have satisfied Jesus as a way of entrance into His kingdom. He will settle for nothing less than making Him the ruler of our lives, with the inevitable result of a practical day-by-day obedience.

PLIABLE AND OBEDIENT

I have no greater joy than to
hear that my children walk in truth.

3 JOHN 1:4

*T*he other day I discovered that I had departed from the habit of looking directly to Jesus for the answer to small daily decisions. The only way I will keep a pliable, obedient spirit in the larger decisions, is to look to Him and *obey* Him in the smaller ones.

Or to approach all this another way, I see that Satan has small chance of getting at us—of accusing us and destroying our rest (as he has with me so often over "small" things like sleeping pills)—when we are faithful in present-moment obedience, steadily looking to Jesus, asking, "Shall I do this? Or not?"—and then obeying.

This obedience *results* in liberty—and the two go hand in hand.

GOD IS LOVE

The LORD is near to all who call upon Him,
to all who call upon Him in truth.

PSALM 145:18

Here are three valid checks for God's guidance: God is love, so He will not tell us to do anything unloving.

God cares about other people as much as He cares about us, so He will not tell us to do something selfish or harmful to others. His true guidance works for the benefit of all persons concerned.

God is righteous, so He will not guide us to any impure act or dishonest act.

Do not rule out God's help with the smallest details of life. After all, details make up the totality of life. If we do not let God into our everyday lives, He may not be able to intervene in the crises.

DENY YOURSELF

If anyone desires to come after Me,
let him deny himself, and take up his cross, and follow Me.

MATTHEW 16:24

Last night at bedtime I ate several pieces of candy, which was wrong from every point of view: pure gratification of momentary desire.

This morning I could not worship the Lord. Something was coming between us. Then the Spirit spoke gently, *"Deny yourself . . . pick up your cross daily and follow Me."* It was as if He were putting His finger on the words "Deny yourself." . . . I looked up the verse and got insight on the rest of the passage: "For whoever wants to save his [higher, spiritual, eternal] life, will lose [the lower, natural, temporal life which is lived (only) on earth]" (Mark 8:35, AMP).

I saw that Jesus is here simply stating a fact of life. If I want to lose weight, I must give up the lower desire for stuffing my mouth in order to attain the higher desire of a fit, healthy body. . . . If I want to write a book, I must give up the use of my time for other things. . . . Lord, teach me!

ACTIVE AND FLEXIBLE

*Do not be unwise, but understand
what the will of the Lord is.*

EPHESIANS 5:17

I like my ruts. But God wants me active, and above all, flexible. . . . So He began teaching me about *how* He goes about changing long-standing habits. It's part of the outworking of His great promise: "This is the covenant that I will make . . . , says the LORD: I will put My law in their minds and write it on their hearts . . ." (Jer. 31:33).

I had never before tied this promise to the problems connected with habit changing. . . . But I see now how He helps us with these ingrained patterns when we ask Him for help. What happens is that *our* tastes begin to change. Something that we liked a lot suddenly is not so appealing. . . .

It's a marvelous plan only He could have thought of, for there is no pain in ceasing to do what we no longer care to do.

A FRIVOLOUS FOCUS?

*Do not love or cherish the world or the things
that are in the world. If any one loves the world,
love for the Father is not in him.*

1 JOHN 2:15–17, AMP

One day a check for several hundred dollars arrived that I hadn't expected. "Now I can get those gold earrings," I said to myself. So I began making trips to jewelry stores looking for the exactly right earrings. Then an inner restlessness began to ruffle me. So I started to argue with God. "Lord, are You telling me that earrings are too frivolous?"

Then came the gentle response: *"I'm concerned over the inordinate amount of time you've given to this in your thought life."*

At once I was led to the apostle John's comment on worldliness and his warning about the "delight of the eyes" in 1 John 2:15. John doesn't use the word "sin"; he doesn't mention Satan. He's concerned with whether we realize the extent of God's love for us—and how much love for God there is in us. . . . The crux of it: the love exchange between God and me is going to suffer if I focus too much on worldly things.

THE BIBLE—OUR TEXTBOOK

He calls his own sheep by name and leads them out.

nyone who means business about God's leading will need to turn again and again to the Bible as a textbook. There are several reasons why this is important. We cannot really know what God is like until we know how God incarnate in human flesh acted, what Jesus' attitude was and is with regard to every facet of the human experience—sin, sickness, disasters, and so on. For this we have to study the Bible intelligently, not as if the Scriptures were a sort of holy rabbit's foot, but for its wisdom in the broad sweep of its teaching about the nature of God and of man.

Then too, the Bible has more explicit guidance for us than most of us are willing to obey. It gives clear directions about money, lawsuits, . . . marriage and divorce, the discipline of children . . . and much more.

GOD'S PERFECT PLAN

We know that all things work together for good
to those who love God, to those who are the called
according to His purpose.

ROMANS 8:28

As long as we maintain our dependence on God, He is able to take all the evils that befall us and weave them into His master plan. Our omnipotent God can make even "the wrath of man to praise Him." He can take any sins, any evil, any calamity—no matter where it originated—and make it "work together for good to those who love God." This practical omnipotence of God is the consistent cry of all of Scripture, written by a variety of men over a period of some thirteen hundred years.

It was also the viewpoint of Jesus. That black moment in the Garden under the olive trees when Judas betrayed his Master with a kiss appeared to be the opening scene in a drama written, staged, and directed by the powers of evil. . . .

"Not so," was Jesus' assertion. Never for an instant during the acting out of that drama did God abdicate as sovereign ruler.

APPROVED BY GOD

The fear of man brings a snare,
but whoever trusts in the LORD shall be safe.

PROVERBS 29:25

I don't fear man in a physical way, but do I fear his disapproval of me? In other words, how much do I try to please other people instead of looking to God alone for His approval? Certainly, there's enormous pressure on all of us to be accepted and approved by others. But God wants us to resist this pressure.

We are told that in our daily task—whatever our vocation or profession or daily round—we are to seek to please God more than man: "Whatever you do, do it heartily, as to the Lord and not to men" (Col. 3:23).

LET CHRIST RULE

You died, and your life is hidden with Christ in God.
COLOSSIANS 3:3, MOFFAT

The matter of getting rid of the old tyrant of self is a deliberate step. I've worked out a plan for ego-slaying that goes something like this:

1. We see the limitation of self-centered living and the danger of it in every area.
2. We pass sentence on the natural self by telling God that we are willing to have Him slay it. Our statement of willingness is a definite act at a given time.
3. We accept by faith the fact that God has heard us; that the next action will be His. . . .
4. Every day of our lives we shall still have to choose between selfishness and unselfishness. But the big decision to let Christ rather than self rule makes all the smaller decisions easier.

MY WILL OR GOD'S WILL?

Whoever abides in Him does not sin.

1 JOHN 3:6

THE EGOCENTRIC PERSONALITY	THE GOD–CENTERED PERSONALITY
*"**M**y will be done."*	*"**T**hy will be done."*
Is intent on self glory.	**H**as true humility.
Is concerned about other people's opinions of self; craves admiration and popularity.	**I**s increasingly free from the necessity for the approval or praise of others.
Is rigid, self-opinionated.	**I**s flexible.
Cannot stand criticism.	**H**andles criticism objectively; usually benefits from it.
Desires power over others; uses others for his own ends.	**I**s devoted to the common good.
Is oversensitive; feelings easily hurt; nourishes resentments.	**R**eadily forgives others.

JUDGING DRAWS JUDGMENT

With what judgment you judge, you will be judged.

MATTHEW 7:2

Being judgmental is an attempt to ward off a fear of criticism by placing one's self in a superior place. Self thinks that when it can get there first and judge before others can state their opinions, it will forestall the criticism of others. Of course, self is mistaken, since the very opposite happens—judging draws the judgment of others.

Two passages of Scripture, personalized for this specific fear, are helping me overcome my exaggerated concern for the approval of others: "Fear not [the opinions of others]: for I have redeemed you; I have called you by your name; you are Mine. When you pass through the waters [of ridicule], I will be with you; and through the rivers [of rejection], they shall not overflow you. When you walk through the fire [of contempt], you shall not be burned, nor shall the flame scorch you" (Isa. 43:1–2).

July

God wants us to catch from Him

some of His vision for us.

RESPECTED AND BELOVED

Let each one of you in particular so love his own wife as himself,
and let the wife see that she respects her husband.

EPHESIANS 5:33

*I*n the countries around the Mediterranean
basin of Paul's day, wives had no political or social
status whatever, were allowed no education, no activity
beyond the home. In the Greek world, for instance, groups of
single young women were trained to provide the social and sex
life of Greek husbands whose wives stayed at home, did the
menial tasks, and cared for the children.

Paul is speaking out against this immoral system and trying
to teach new Ephesian Christians how they should relate to one
another. It is only against this pagan backdrop that we can see
how revolutionary Paul's "Husbands, love your wives" was! Not
only was Paul not against women, he, like his Master before
him, was teaching that women are equally children of the
Father and as such are to be respected and beloved. At that time,
a radically new approach to women!

THE GLORY OF CHRIST

You are worthy, O Lord, to receive glory
and honor and power; for You created all things,
and by Your will they exist and were created.

REVELATION 4:11

The glory of Jesus Christ lies in the characteristics of His nature that make us want to adore Him. These traits are not the kingly trappings or the halo placed around His head by medieval painters. Far from it! Men saw His glory in His humanity—His instant compassion, tenderness, understanding, fearlessness, incisiveness, His refusal to compromise with evil, and His selflessness, which culminated in His ultimate self-giving on the cross.

The apostle John puts it in unforgettable words: "And the Word became flesh and dwelt among us, and we beheld His glory as of the only begotten of the Father, full of grace and truth" (John 1:14).

GIVING GRACE IN LOVE

Who is he who condemns? It is Christ who died,
and . . . is also risen, . . . who also makes intercession for us.

ROMANS 8:34

he apostle, Paul, waxed lyrical about the great truth of God's grace. No doubt because he, even more than most of us, had tried so hard to be his own savior—and had failed. And so he exults . . . "When God acquits, who shall condemn?"

How much we need this lack of condemnation, all of us. And when finally we are able to accept grace and to realize it in ourselves, then (at last) we are able to help others around us to receive it. We can give them, too, the chance to be themselves, to find themselves, and even to find their own way to God. Only then do we discover that grace in love is the adhesive that mends every broken relationship.

THE RIGHT TO HAPPINESS?

Whoever trusts in the LORD, happy is he.

PROVERBS 16:20

ddly our national preoccupation with happiness was clearly stated in the Declaration of Independence: "We hold these truths to be self-evident that all men are . . . endowed by their Creator with certain unalienable rights, that among these are life, liberty, and the pursuit of happiness." . . .

The truth, as I see it, is that not one of us has "an unalienable right" to anything, not even to life itself. We did not ask to be born and we are dependent for the next breath we draw on the grace of God. How arrogant and ungrateful we must seem to our Creator when we demand our "rights"—particularly when we have given nothing of ourselves to Him.

A PERFECT FIT

*Take My yoke upon you and learn from Me, for I am
gentle and lowly in heart, and you will find rest for your souls.
For My yoke is easy and My burden is light.*

MATTHEW 11:29–30

I was given a whole new perception of these verses through my friend, Roberta.

She had always thought of these verses in Matthew as a metaphor of Jesus helping her with *her* projects, *her* life—plowing *her* field, so to speak.

Then one day the Lord said to her something like this: "No, you have it all wrong—backwards. Drop your plans. At the beginning of each day simply ask to be yoked with Me for *My* work, to plow *My* field. Then you will find that the yoke fits perfectly and that the burden truly is light."

PRAISE FOR ALL THINGS

In everything give thanks; for this is the will
of God in Christ Jesus for you.

1 THESSALONIANS 5:18

How can I deal with resentments that smolder inside me? The verse above holds the answer. I am to praise God for *all* things, regardless of where they seem to originate. Doing this, He points out, is the key to receiving the blessings of God. Praise will wash away my resentments. I've known this, accepted it, even written about it. But as I began praising Him yesterday, my efforts were wooden.

Then came these thoughts: I was to ignore my *feelings* and act on the *principle*. I was to do it despite the lack of joy—simply because God told me to. True praise grows out of the recognition and acknowledgment that in His time God will bring good out of bad. There is the intolerable situation on the one hand and the fulfillment of Romans 8:28 on the other hand. ("All things work together for good. . . .")

THE STILL SMALL VOICE

If you are willing and obedient,
you shall eat the good of the land.

ISAIAH 1:19

received a letter from a young lady who had decided not to leave the matter of finding the right husband to "chance." Statistics showed there were more single men in the West, so she decided the intelligent thing to do was to go west. But before doing that she decided to pray about such a drastic decision. "Lord, you know what my real desire is. What do *You* want me to do in getting this heart's desire?"

Very clearly, she felt God spoke to her heart. "I want you to act out your faith by staying right where you are. I can handle the matter of providing a husband for you."

It seemed rather undramatic, but she set her will to obey the still small voice. After that she discovered in herself a new kind of belief and trust that God really would answer her prayer. . . . Just three months later she met her future husband in a restaurant in her hometown!

LIKE A CHILD

The wisdom of this world is foolishness with God.

1 CORINTHIANS 3:19

gain I'm back to relinquishment. Time after time I've laid my concerns, questions, doubts, plans, on God's altar. The problem for me is leaving them there.

At age sixty-five I still have that determination to take charge of my life, to prove that I can still do everything I did when I was twenty. I still want God to applaud my good works. It's so ridiculous! . . .

Meanwhile, God waits patiently for me to come to Him, forgetting my own agenda, so that I can hear what He has in mind for me.

Is it possible for an opinionated woman in her autumn years to become like a child and sit at the feet of Jesus with one idea—to hear what He will say?

WHAT PEACE WE FORFEIT

I, even I, am He who comforts you.
Who are you that you should be afraid . . . ?

ISAIAH 51:12

Knowing that all people struggle with fear, Jesus often prefaced what He was about to say to His fellow humans with the words, "Fear not." Therefore my prayer is, "Lord, I hand my fears over to You, fears of all kinds. Fear of You is actually a kind of blasphemy against Your character. I'm sorry. Forgive me."

In answer to my prayer, a line from an old hymn began running through my mind. The Spirit said very clearly, "*Pay attention to every line of these verses. Learn to bring everything directly to Me instead of allowing so many worrying wonderings*".

> *O what peace we often forfeit,*
> *O what needless pain we bear,*
> *All because we do not carry*
> *Everything to God in prayer.*

—JOSEPH SCRIVEN (1819–1886)

God's Glorious Grace

My grace is sufficient for you,
for My strength is made perfect in weakness.

2 CORINTHIANS 12:9

o save us from eternal death, God sent Jesus to live among us and demonstrate personally that His love has no conditions; it includes every human being. Somewhere in the procession of men and women who touched Him, each of us will find ourselves:

> to the socialite, Levi, Jesus extended his friendship;
> to the man with a sick mind who lived among the tombs, He gave healing;
> to the woman taken in adultery, He offered love and [forgiveness];
> to Zacchaeus, who loved money, He offered companion ship and a new set of priorities.

Seeing this unconditional love, reveling in the glory of it, the New Testament writers were forced to coin a word to describe it—*grace*. For them grace meant the safety and acceptance by God they could not earn and only Christ could provide.

PERFECT CONFIDENCE

Beloved, let us love one another, for love is of God.

1 JOHN 4:7

have come to believe that only if we can depend upon the Creator as a God of love (not an obscure, ethereal love, but love as you and I know it) shall we have the courage and confidence to turn our life and affairs over to Him. Hannah Smith once wrote this pithy sentence: "Perfect obedience would be perfect happiness, if only we had perfect confidence in the power we were obeying."

What builds trust like that in the Creator? Only knowing Him well—His motives, His complete goodwill—and being certain that no pressures will make Him change.

JUDGE NOT

Judge not, that you be not judged.

MATTHEW 7:1

ll through the Sermon on the Mount, Jesus sets Himself squarely against our seeing other people and life situations through a negative, critical lens. What He is showing me so far can be summed up as follows:

1. A critical spirit focuses us on ourselves and makes us unhappy. We lose perspective and humor.
2. A critical spirit blocks the positive creative thoughts God longs to give us.
3. A critical spirit can prevent good relationships between individuals and often produces retaliatory criticalness.
4. Criticalness blocks the work of the Spirit of God: love, goodwill, mercy.

Whenever we see something genuinely wrong in people's behavior, rather than criticize them directly, or—far worse—gripe about them behind their back, we should ask the Spirit of God to do the correction needed.

A MAGNET FOR GOD'S POWER

Be strong in the Lord and in the power of His might.

EPHESIANS 6:10

Discouragement says, "My problem is bigger than God, who is not adequate to handle my particular need. So herewith I take my eyes off God, bow down before my problem, and give myself to it."

In digging through Scripture on this subject, I have discovered that no matter how difficult the situation, Jesus' attitude was always a calm, "Courage, My son, My daughter. Have no fear. There is nothing here that My Father cannot handle."

It was not that Jesus minimized the problem, but rather that His faith was a magnet for God's power. He knew that *no* problem was any match for the Lord God Almighty.

OUR BURDEN-BEARER

Casting all your care upon Him, for He cares for you.

1 PETER 5:7

*S*ome time ago a good friend spoke to me of her burden. Her older son was estranged from her. He had written her a terse, shattering letter cutting off all communication. "Don't even send me a Christmas card or a birthday card," he wrote.

"The New Testament has good news in a case like this," I told her. "Jesus came to earth for the specific purpose of being our Burden-Bearer. He wants to take over 'the government' of our lives. This isn't any risk for us because He's all love, all good will, all unselfishness. So why don't you simply tell Him that this problem is too much for you, that you want Him to take over the government of your life, including this—and He will."

My friend did just that. She relinquished the whole problem to Jesus. . . . A year and a half later, the son came to see her. All was forgiven. Today, mother and son, new wife, and baby boy have a great relationship.

GOD WORKS ON THE ESCAPE

God has not given us a spirit of fear,
but of power and of love and of a sound mind.

2 TIMOTHY 1:7

s Abraham and Isaac were toiling up Mount Moriah, Satan must have been tempting Abraham every few minutes. "Surely you did not hear God correctly! Sacrifice your son and heir? Why should you do such an evil thing? Why, Isaac was God's special gift to you in your wife's old age. You're probably just getting senile," and so forth.

But at *the very moment* Abraham was struggling with his thoughts, the ram was traveling up the *other* side of the Mount, and God was preparing the way of escape.

The message? God is always working on the "ram part"—the escape, His own way out.

SIN STRIKES OUT

The Lord knows how to
deliver the godly out of temptations.

2 PETER 2:9

How much better we will withstand Satan's assaults when we're wise to his tactics! . . . I've been searching the Bible for insights as to the forces . . . arrayed against us.

The Serpent's Strategy:

First of all the serpent's objective was to call God a liar, to contradict His Word, to tell Eve—and us—"His Word is not so." It was because Eve believed the serpent as over against God that the Fall came (Gen. 3:2–4).

The serpent's second strategy was to tell Eve, in effect, "God is out to take away or withhold something good from you."

The third trick was to tempt the woman into letting the forbidden fruit play upon her senses. She put herself in the way of the temptation, walked around it, looked at it, toyed with it (Gen. 3:6).

Three curve balls—and Eve struck out.

THE LION OF JUDAH

Your adversary the devil walks about like a roaring lion,
seeking whom he may devour.

1 PETER 5:8

Peter did not write those words to scare us to death. For the key word is *like* a lion. Satan is always an imitator, a fake, a bluff, a counterfeit. He *isn't* a lion. His claws were drawn out at Calvary.

The real Lion is Jesus, "the Lion of the tribe of Judah" (Rev. 5:5). We Christians have no strength or ability in ourselves for fighting Satan, or for pulling down gates, or anything else.

But as we allow the Lion of Judah to live in us, we take on the nature of Him who is the real Lion. Our weapons—fickle and weak of themselves—pass through God and become mighty enough to make hell itself tremble with fear.

GOD INHABITS OUR PRAISES

My soul shall be joyful in the LORD;
it shall rejoice in His salvation.

PSALM 35:9

A new book came in the mail one day: *Prison to Praise* by former Army chaplain, Merlin Carothers. The author's thesis is that God steps in to change unhappy or even disastrous situations in our lives when we thank Him *for the situation itself.* This makes sense only when we see that life as it comes to each of us day by day is our schoolroom. That, in turn, can be true only when we at last understand that God is "in" every circumstance—good or bad—that He allows to come to us.

Growth comes ... when we take an active step toward God, who stands waiting for us at the center of the problem. The quickest way to go to meet Him is through praise. No wonder we meet Him there, for Scripture goes on to teach us that God actually "inhabits" (lives in) the praises of His people (Ps. 22:3).

REGRETS ARE A WASTE OF TIME

Great peace have those who love Your law,
and nothing causes them to stumble.

PSALM 119:165

rother Lawrence once said that he was never upset when he had failed in some duty. He simply confessed his fault, saying to God, "I shall never do otherwise, if You leave me to myself; it is You who must hinder my failing and mend what is amiss." After this admission, he gave himself no further uneasiness about it.

What the devil wants us to do, of course, is to focus on our failure rather than on Jesus. For when we keep our eyes on Him, we find that no problem—of the first century or the twentieth—has ever defeated Him.

LIGHT AND LIFE

In Him was life, and the life was the light of men.

JOHN 1:4

There's a close relation between God as light and God as life. In the first chapter of his gospel, John makes these assertions:

Christ, as God Himself, is the light of men (vs. 4).

Every man who comes into this world, is born with Christ's light in his being (vs. 9).

Hence, possessing that light and becoming a son of God are quite different. We have no choice about the former; the latter is dependent upon our free-will (vs. 9, 12, 13).

Intelligence, health, kindness, love, compassion, unselfishness, happiness are all part of God's light and life, and are God's good gifts to mankind. Derangement, disease, harshness, hate, selfishness, depression, and darkness result from misusing the gift of light and life given to us at birth.

Let's consider what we can do to increase God's light and life in ourselves.

CHRIST AT LIFE'S CENTER

Not everyone who says to me, "Lord, Lord,"
shall enter the kingdom of heaven, but he who does
the will of My Father in heaven.

MATTHEW 7:21

If the idea of Christ living at the center of life frightens us, it may be because we fear that by handing over self-will we would then become spineless creatures, colorless carbon-copy personalities. We need not be afraid on either count. Actually, it's when selfishness and self-will progressively take over in our society that we become carbon copies of one another. When people are not in the least concerned about pleasing God, they are desperately concerned about pleasing each other. . . .

Whenever we exchange self-will for God's will, we find greater strength, a finer quality of iron in the new will given us. And, by a strange paradox, we then become more individualistic, with more unique personalities than we would have thought possible. That is because we have exchanged the mask for the real self.

THE TREASURY OF HEAVEN

So I tell you, whatever you pray for and ask,
believe that you have got it and you shall have it.

MARK 11:24

Is there a contradiction in the verb tenses of this verse? How *can* we believe that we already possess something promised to us for the future?

Yet this puzzling promise contains a priceless spiritual law. You and I see time as divided between past, present, and future only because we are finite. With God, there is only the infinite NOW. Therefore, by faith we must grasp the fact that all the blessings we shall ever need are already deposited in the Treasury of Heaven.

Money in any checking account will stay right there until the owner cashes a check *in the present.* Even so, we shall receive God's blessings only as we claim them one by one *in the present.* Faith in the future tense is hope—not faith. Nor will we keep asking for what we already have. A sure sign that our hope has passed into faith is when we stop begging God and begin thanking Him for the answer to our prayer.

GIVE US MORE FAITH!

Without faith it is impossible to please Him.

HEBREWS 11:6

One day the apostles cried as with one voice to Jesus. "Give us more faith." They saw this as the most urgent need of their lives. What was it in Jesus' attitude that caused them to make this poignant appeal?

As He healed the diseased and the maimed, Jesus kept telling the sufferers that their recovery depended upon their faith (Luke 8:18, 50; Matt. 9:29). As He forgave sins, He said that forgiveness depended on faith (Luke 5:20; 7:50). As He controlled the elements of nature, He asked His disciples, "Where is your faith?" (Luke 8:25). Jesus' one fear about His second coming seemed to be that He might not find faith on the earth (Luke 18:8). . . . No wonder Christians, then and now, have pleaded, "Give us more faith!"

A PERMANENT JOY

You shall go out with joy, and be led out with peace.

ISAIAH 55:12

The process of being molded into a mature person in Christ Jesus becomes more challenging with each year that passes. I am finding that the knowledge of God grows often by means of the very experiences that would sweep me downstream, the turbulence I would prefer to escape.

As we grow older, the pace and dimension of physical life must wind down. But it is meant to be just the opposite with the spiritual life—growth at an ever-accelerating pace. The heights and depths of the spirit, and enthusiasm for God aren't for children. In the latter half of life the normal Christian almost breaks into a jog or a run. Excitement and aliveness build. An altogether new quality of joy is given to us. It has little to do with the circumstances of our lives—good or bad—but everything to do with knowing Him who is managing the circumstances. It is joy that has the feel of permanence, even of eternity about it.

HELPING CHRIST HELP OTHERS

He has sent Me to heal the brokenhearted,
to proclaim liberty to the captives . . .
to set at liberty those who are oppressed.

LUKE 4:18

he Gospel accounts show Christ with a passion for helping those in trouble. He has not changed! The minute we need saving from anything, He stands ready in His role as Savior.

And when we minister to someone hungry or poverty-stricken or ill or in prison, we are ministering to Him. (Matt. 25:37–46) When we persecute others, we persecute Jesus. (Acts 9:4–5) When we receive and welcome one little child, we receive and welcome Him.(Mark 9:36–37)

Frank Laubach has put this in a memorable way: "At the center of every need He stands pleading with us to help Him as He moved to help others". He is not only "in" trouble and sorrow, but is there in a particular way—to have dialogue with us, to teach us, and then to rescue us.

EYES OF COMPASSION

In lowliness of mind let each esteem others better than himself.

PHILIPPIANS 2:3

still have a bad attitude toward a woman who is constantly attacking me and my writings. On taking it to the Lord, I received two insights.

The reason I am so upset is that *I haven't forgiven her completely.* I've made stabs at this in the past, but as she comes to my mind I have an almost physical sensation of iron bars pressing against my chest. The Lord showed me that on the other side of these bars was a woman, a human being, who needed to be freed. So . . . I went through a process of unreservedly forgiving her by an act of my will. I confessed my feelings about her and asked God to make the forgiveness real.

My job was not finished, however, He told me, until *I could forget what she had done.* . . . I was to ask forgiveness for hanging onto these memories . . . and ask for an alarm system on the door of my mind whenever the memory tries to creep back. From henceforth I am to look at this woman with eyes of compassion and love.

FREEDOM OF WILL

I stand at the door and knock.
If anyone hears My voice and opens the door,
I will come in to him and dine with him, and he with me.

REVELATION 3:20

The Christian life must be lived in the will, not in the emotions. God regards the decisions and choices of a person's will as the decisions and choices of the person himself—no matter how contrary the emotions may be. Moreover, when this principle is applied, the emotions must always capitulate to the will. . . .

At birth, God gives each human being the gift of freedom of will. Under no circumstances will God ever violate this central citadel of man's being. The picture in the book of Revelation of Christ standing, knocking, outside the closed door of the human heart, I believe to be a literal picture. . . .

The latch of the door is on the inside. It is our hand that must open the door. It is our voice that must invite Christ in.

WALKING BY FAITH

That we who first trusted in Christ
should be to the praise of His glory.

EPHESIANS 1:12

Every time we eat a meal in a restaurant we trust some unknown cook behind the scenes and we eat the food on faith—faith that it is not contaminated.... We accept a prescription from a doctor and take it to a pharmacist, thus acting on faith that the pharmacist will fill the prescription accurately.... It is obvious that were we to insist on the "proof first, then faith" order in our daily lives, organized life as we know it would grind to a screeching halt....

The New Testament makes it clear that in the spiritual realm, when for some reason or other we refuse to act by faith, all activity stops just as completely as it does in the secular realm. There is no way for us even to take the first steps toward the Christian life except by faith.... Every step in our Christian walk has to be by faith.

GOD IN EVERYTHING

Are not two sparrows sold for a copper coin?
And not one of them falls to the ground apart from your Father's will. . . .
Do not fear therefore; you are of more value than many sparrows.

MATTHEW 10:29–31

In the verse above Jesus was telling us that since not even one insignificant sparrow can perish without the knowledge and consent of a loving Father, and, more, His participating presence (since He stands waiting at the center of every need), then we should have no fear. Each of us is infinitely precious in the Father's sight, so much so that He knows every detail about us, even to the number of the hairs on our head.

Therefore, nothing can happen to us without His knowledge, His consent, and *His participating presence* as Savior. This is what we mean by God being "in everything."

A Sacrifice of Praise

Let us continually offer the sacrifice of praise to God,
that is, the fruit of our lips, giving thanks to His name.

HEBREWS 13:15

The fact that the word *sacrifice* is used [in this verse] tells us the writers of Scripture understood well that when we praise God for trouble, we're giving up something. For sacrifice means "the surrender or destruction of something prized or desirable for the sake of something considered as having a higher or more pressing claim." What we're sacrificing is the right to the blessings we think are due us!

We are also sacrificing our human desire to understand everything. Obviously, praising God for trouble makes no sense from the earthly side. Human reason asks, "Why should I thank God for dark and negative circumstances when He is the Author of light and goodness alone?" So when we bypass our "right" to understand and offer up suffering to God in praise, the Bible is right in calling this a "sacrifice of praise."

CONSISTENT COMMUNICATION

And whatever you do, do it heartily,
as to the Lord and not to men.

COLOSSIANS 3:23

God's guidance will never contradict itself. That is, He will not give us a direction through the inner voice of the Holy Spirit that will ever contradict . . . the Scriptures.

Hannah Whitehall Smith cited a humorous example of this. A woman once stole some money because she had opened her Bible at random and put her finger on 1 Corinthians 3:21: " . . . For all things are yours. . . ." Obviously the woman would have done better to consider the consistent voice of Scripture on the side of total honesty, and its thundering "thou shall not steal."

The point is that, in the main, the Bible deals in principles—not disjointed aphorisms or superficial rules of conduct.

August

Obey God one step at a time,

then the next step will come into view.

BLACK AND WHITE

Happy are the people whose God is the LORD!

PSALM 144:15

od's Presence can be the catalyst to turn evil events and situations into good ones. We could compare it to the process that a photographer goes through to develop a negative into a beautiful print. (The word "negative" is intriguing here.) When we hold a photo negative up to a light, all objects are reversed: black is white, white is black. Further, the character lineaments of any face in the picture are not clear.

Once plunged into the developing solution, what photographers call "the latent image" is revealed in the print—darkness turns to light and lo, we have a beautiful picture. . . .

When we praise God by an act of the will . . . , first we accept present circumstances, then we take up a positive position. By beginning to praise Him for the evil, we take our less-than-good situation and plunge in into the photographer's fluid—the presence of God.

ANYTHING AGAINST ANYONE

If you forgive men their trespasses,
your heavenly Father will also forgive you.

MATTHEW 6:14

Most of us are aware that Christ requires us to forgive. Yet forgiving is not easy when the other person is clearly in the wrong. This is especially true in actions that violate God's and man's laws and the good that God wants for His world . . .

For years I attached a condition to my forgiveness: if the other person saw the error of his ways, was properly sorry, and admitted his guilt, then yes, as a Christian, I was obligated to forgive him. Finally I had to face the fact that this was *my* set of conditions, not Christ's. For He said, "If you have anything against anyone, forgive him . . ." (Mark 11:25). "Anyone" can have only one meaning: anybody-everybody-all-inclusive. As for the particular wrongs we are to forgive, Jesus is just as demanding on us there. His instructions are to forgive "anything." The dictionary definition of "anything" is "any thing whatever." Again, all-inclusive.

WITHHOLDING JUDGMENT

Whatever you bind on earth will be bound in heaven,
and whatever you loose on earth will be loosed in heaven.

MATTHEW 18:18

For a long time I was puzzled," our friend David told us, "about what 'loosing' and 'binding' meant in Matthew chapter eighteen. Then I found out it means that by hanging onto my judgment of another, I can bind that person to the very conditions I'd like to see changed.

"By our unforgiveness, we stand between the other person and the Holy Spirit's work in convicting him and then helping him. By stepping out of the way through releasing somebody from our judgment, we're not necessarily saying, 'He's right and I'm wrong'. Forgiveness means, 'He can be as wrong as wrong can be, but I'll not be the judge'. Forgiveness means that I'm no longer binding a certain person on earth. It means withholding judgment."

LOOK FEAR IN THE FACE

There is no fear in love;
but perfect love casts out fear,
because fear involves torment.

1 JOHN 4:18

ear is like a screen erected between God and us, so that His power cannot get through to us. So, how do we get rid of fear?

This is not easy when the life of someone dear hangs in the balance, or when what we want most is involved. At such times, every emotion, every passion, is tied up in the dread that what we fear most is about to come upon us. Obviously only drastic measures can deal with such a gigantic fear and the demanding spirit that usually goes along with it. . . .

Jesus says, admit the possibility of what you fear most. And lo, as you stop fleeing, force yourself to walk up to the fear, look it full in the face—never forgetting that God and His power are still the supreme reality—and the fear evaporates. Drastic? Yes. But it is one sure way of releasing prayer power into human affairs.

THE RUDDER OF LIFE

Speaking the truth in love . . .
grow up in all things into Him who is the head—Christ.

EPHESIANS 4:15

We forgive others by our wills—the rudders of our lives. We are responsible for the set of this rudder. Then once we have willed a course of action, God will be responsible for our feelings if we will hand them over to Him. Otherwise, nothing we can do would change these feelings.

I put that conclusion alongside a statement by David du Plessis: "Forgiveness means, the other person may be as wrong as wrong can be, but I'll not be the judge." Then I see that forgiveness is simply the decision of our wills to release a particular person, followed by verbalizing that to God. It can be a simple prayer like, "Lord, I release _____ from my judgment. Forgive me that I may have bound _____ and hampered Your work by judging. Now I step out of the way so that Heaven can go into action for _____."

Obviously, there is nothing impossible about praying like that.

LIFE FOR DEATH

Whoever calls on the name of the Lord shall be saved.

ACTS 2:21

As a result of man's disobedience, death entered life, precisely as God had said it would. Not just the cessation of the heartbeat and the decay of the flesh that marks the end of life, but all the interim ills that lead up to death—sickness, disease, pain . . . famine, pestilence, plague, fear, loneliness, hatred, jealousy, hurt, cruelty, torture, murder, suicide. Now began the long history of man's inhumanity to man—man now bound tightly, stultified by the fallen divided nature that he himself had chosen. . . .

But it did not end that way.

Jesus' death and resurrection was the Master Plan to win back for man all that he had lost in Eden. As the last Adam, Jesus would mount His cross taking all of us, Adam's heirs, with Him into the death of the old, now-spoiled creation. Thus He would accomplish a perfect exchange.

DECIDING FOR CHRIST

You, LORD, are good, and ready to forgive,
and abundant in mercy to all those who call upon You.

PSALM 86:5

Whether we are millionaires directing a financial kingdom or youthful idealists in revolt against a materialistic world, or quite ordinary citizens content to live self-centered lives of quiet mediocrity, until such time as we get reconnected to Life, we remain vulnerable to Satan's cunning approach and to his designs. Each of us can escape the bondage of Satan's kingdom for the freedom of Christ's kingdom only when we resolutely set the rudder of our wills to do so.

That's why the moment of decision for Christ is so vital. That's why the angels themselves rejoice when even one lost lamb is brought back on the shoulder of the Good Shepherd.

THE SOURCE OF SELF-PITY

The LORD will give strength to His people,
the LORD will bless His people with peace.

PSALM 29:11

After we become Christians, Satan's aim is to oppose and stymie us so that our spirits will be stunted short of maturity. He also wants to keep us ineffective so far as spreading to others the good news of freedom in Christ Jesus.

An endlessly used weapon in his spiritual arsenal is that of discouragement, often interlocked with a degree of self-pity and depression. During our early years in Washington when Peter Marshall often battled discouragement, I remember our quoting at one another one of Hannah Smith's favorite maxims: "All discouragement is of the devil." Of course the remedy is to realize the source of the depression and to remind oneself that spiritual reality can never be gauged by feelings.

CHOOSING WHAT IS BEST

*Your word is a lamp to my feet
and a light to my path.*

PSALM 119:105

SATAN'S DESIRES

Wants us to live in darkness and hide portions of our life from others.

Wants us to doubt and disbelieve God's word.

Works to make us ignore, disbelieve, or choose for ourselves what to believe in the Scripture.

Pushes us to disobey God.

JESUS' DESIRES

Wants us to live in the light.

Longs for us to have faith that He always keeps His word.

Steadily assures us that the Scripture is the Word of God.

Says, "If you love Me, you will obey my commandments."

ONE CHOICE LEADS TO ANOTHER

He who does the truth comes to the light,
that his deeds may be clearly seen, that they have been done in God.

JOHN 3:20–21

We are creatures of habit patterns for good or ill. In other words, we do not make a series of equal and independent decisions, rather one decision leads to another. Unfortunately, the natural inclination we have inherited from our father Adam toward making the wrong choice means that this phenomenon works more easily downward than upward. Any parent or teacher concerned with children knows this well. For instance, it is easier to let a child be sloppy and to allow careless habits to develop than it is to fight uphill toward his becoming an ordered, neat person. Moreover, each repetition of a downbeat choice makes the next one easier and bothers us less as sin's inevitable deadening process sets in.

WE'RE NOT SUNK

Having wiped out the handwriting of requirements that was against us . . .
He has taken it out of the way, having nailed it to the cross.

COLOSSIANS 2:14

I remember how Peter Marshall once made this truth real and personal. One evening a friend had questioned him about God's judgment. Did he really think that there was going to be an accounting for each of us?

"Yes, I do think so," Peter answered promptly. "The Bible makes it quite clear. I think I may have to go through the agony of having Old Scratch, the accuser, recite my sins in the presence of God.

"But I believe it will be like this: Jesus, our High Priest, will come over and lay His hand across my shoulders and say to God, 'Yes, all these things are true, but I'm here to cover up for Peter. He is sorry for all his sins, and by a transaction made between us, I am now solely responsible for them.'"

Suddenly Peter smiled. "And, sister, if I'm wrong about that, *I'm sunk.*"

But we're not sunk. Glory be to God!

DELIVERED–NOT DEFEATED

Be diligent to be found by Him in peace,
without spot and blameless.

2 PETER 3:14

THE DEVOURER

Wants us to hang onto resentment and bitterness.

Urges us to have our fun now; try to forget about paying for it.

Attempts to get us to hide our sins and make excuses for them, thus encouraging their festering within.

Wants us, when we fail, to wallow in discouragement or despair.

THE DELIVERER

Tells us to forgive others in the same way God forgives us.

Influences us to pay now in time or effort, then fun later is assured.

Wishes us to run to Him, bring our sins into the light and have them forgiven cleansed, and forgotten.

Encourages us in failure to ask forgiveness, accept it, rise, and go on.

THE GOD OF ALL COMFORT

Blessed be the God and Father of our Lord Jesus Christ,
the Father of mercies and God of all comfort,
Who comforts us in all our affliction.

2 CORINTHIANS 1:3-4 RSV

Do you recall the time Jesus met ten lepers (Luke 17:11–19)? Since lepers were ostracized from public gatherings, these men stood at a distance, crying, "Jesus, Master, have mercy on us."

The Master did not question each man about how well he had kept the Law or how righteous he was. Simply out of Jesus' overflowing, compassionate love, He healed them. "Go and show yourselves to the priests," He told them. And later, "Your faith has restored you to health" (The Amplified Bible).

Faith in what or whom? The connecting link is our belief that God loves each of us with a love more wondrous than the most warmhearted person we know; that He heals simply out of His love and because He wants us to have the joy of abundant health.

HOPE AND TRUST

In You, O LORD, I put my trust;
let me never be put to shame.

PSALM 71:1

Long ago I wrote these words on the flyleaf of a favorite copy of the New Testament: "God specializes in things thought impossible."

Time and experience and hundreds of answers to prayer have undergirded this thought. Faith in God's power is at the heart of Christianity. Nothing else really matters but the question of all questions: Can you and I trust the love and the power of our God?

PUT PEOPLE FIRST

The LORD upholds all who fall,
and raises up all who are bowed down.

PSALM 145:14

A have watched what happens when people make contact with God. First, feeling comes alive, for there can be no fresh life without feeling. The results of this alone are momentous and far-reaching. All true creativity has an emotional base, and women have to find creativity for any self-realization. Then, as feeling comes alive, they come to have that inner warmth that gives them the capacity for loving and being loved.

The next thing that happens when they contact God is that He will insist that they put people, rather than things or ideas, at the center of their lives. "Follow Me, and I will make you fishers of men. . ." is the principle upon which He insists.

WORK DEDICATED TO GOD

Whatever you do, do it heartily,
as to the Lord and not to men.

COLOSSIANS 3:23

urely one of the tragedies of our time is that a highly industrialized and urbanized society has robbed millions of deep vocational satisfaction. God means for us to find the task that gives us the most joy to do. Then His plan is that monetary reward should come to us purely as a dividend.

When we mistakenly put the cart before the horse and pick our jobs primarily for the material rewards, something devastating happens. Some shining quality goes out of work. Then we wonder why life holds so little excitement and why the things that we buy give us limited satisfaction. We forget that "the chief end of man is go glorify God and to enjoy Him forever." And we forget that it is only as we seek to glorify God in our daily work that enjoyment of God and of life, even of ourselves, is possible. . . .

Each of us has daily work. And if you want new zest in life, try the adventure of dedicating that work to God.

EMPTY BEFORE GOD

I will even make a way in the wilderness and rivers in the desert.

ISAIAH 43:19

When Len and I had a preliminary audience with Queen Salote Tupou of Tonga, we were quickly won by her graciousness. Even as a little girl, prayer came to mean to her "personal conversations with Jesus."

"Today, I always begin with silence," she told us, "which is a gathering of my own thoughts and a time of worship of the greatest Person I know. Then quietly I go through a process of emptying myself out before God. If there is grief—and there often has been in my life—I tell of my grief; if there is a problem, I pour out the problem.

"Sometimes in my inadequacy I stand there shivering. So often I've found that I have to come down to complete helplessness before God can get through to me. But He has never failed me. Always there is help, always an answer." The brown eyes became thoughtful, then the Queen chuckled. "Sometimes the answer is not at all what I want to hear."

SPIRITUAL NOURISHMENT

Incline your ear and hear the words of the wise,
and apply your heart to my knowledge.

PROVERBS 22:17

t was one morning in the summer of 1944 that I quietly made an act of handing my life over to God. In the days following that commitment, I became aware of insatiable spiritual hunger. I was as one who had been without food for so long that she was oblivious of her hunger until, in the presence of Christ, suddenly I knew my starvation.

Then a line from the twenty-third Psalm came true for me: "You prepare a table before me . . ."

The table was laden with spiritual food—much of it in the form of books. Foremost were the Scriptures, which suddenly came to life and became manna, nourishment to my spirit. Then there were other books, lots of books. Mostly, they were not theology as such, nor religious theory, nor especially learned, but the simple accounts of how others had contacted God and of how He had dealt with them.

DEEP INNER CHANGES

He has sent Me to heal the brokenhearted,
to proclaim liberty to the captives . . . to set at liberty
those who are oppressed.

LUKE 4:18

*S*atan was the original instigator of rebellion. . . .
He whispers to us that the way to improve our lot is
to rebel.

But . . . what is God's way? That was essentially the question
the thoughtful scholar Nicodemus came asking Jesus during
their quiet midnight talk. The Master's answer was, "Those deep
inner changes are never going to come about through men's
efforts in trying to change the thinking or patch up the old
person. There's only one way, Nicodemus: *'except a man be born*
again, he cannot see the Kingdom of God.'"

And when Nicodemus probed and questioned, "How *can*
these things be?" Jesus pointed him to a cross. How well He knew
that soon He would hang there suspended between earth and
heaven. And there, if we will recognize it and allow it to be so,
our old selves, too, can die so that the new person can be born.

GOD'S FREE GIFTS

To the LORD our God belong
mercy and forgiveness, though we
have rebelled against Him.

DANIEL 9:9

Paul tells us why Jesus did not inquire about the worthiness of those whom He healed or lifted out of sin: "So then (God's gift) is not a question of human will and human effort, but of God's mercy . . ." (Rom. 9:16, AMP). In other words, there is nothing you or I can do to earn God's gifts. We are dependent on His loving mercy.

When I searched out the word "mercy" in Cruden's *Concordance,* I found a surprisingly long list of Scripture references. Moreover, Alexander Cruden's original words of description set down in 1769 are rich food for thought: "Mercy signifies that essential perfection in God, whereby He pities and relieves the miseries of His creatures"; and "'Grace' flows from 'mercy' as its fountain."

THE SPIRIT IS A FRIEND

For as many as are led by the Spirit of God,
these are sons of God.

ROMANS 8:14

Most of us begin by thinking of the Holy Spirit as an influence, something ghostly, ethereal, that produces a warm and loving feeling in us. But the Helper is no influence. He is a Person—one of the three Persons of the Godhead. He possesses all the attributes of personality. He has a mind; He has knowledge; He has a will. We can find biblical backing for all these attributes: He speaks; He prays; He teaches; He commands; He forbids.

Being a Person, the Spirit is a Friend whom we can come to know and to love. One of His most lovable characteristics is that He deliberately submerges Himself in Jesus; He works at being inconspicuous. Always there is a transparency in His personality so that Jesus can shine through. It is the Spirit's specific work to reveal facets of the Lord's personality to us; to woo us and lead us to the Other, to glorify Him, to bring Him and His words to our remembrance.

DON'T MISS THE MESSAGE

I will never leave you nor forsake you.

HEBREWS 13:5

One Sunday when our son was quite young, our whole family, including a small guest of Peter John's, went to a Washington hotel for Sunday dinner. After dinner, Dr. Marshall lingered in the lobby to talk to an acquaintance. The two boys grew restless, and asked to go out into the yard to play. The hotel was set back from the street in the wide lawns, so I let them go. Minutes passed. Then gently, but clearly, that still small Voice gave me a message, "The boys need you. Better go out to them immediately."

I excused myself and went. The two boys were standing hand in hand on the curb just ready to try to cross Sixteenth Street— one of Washington's busiest and most dangerous thoroughfares. Such happenings make me wonder whether the Holy Spirit does not often try to save His children from many of the accidents and disasters of our lives on this earth. But we who do not practice the art of listening to that small Voice.

COMPLETE SURRENDER

God is our refuge and strength,
a very present help in trouble.

PSALM 46:1

od cannot lead the individual who is not willing to give Him a blank check with his life. Telling Christ we are willing to turn our lives over to Him *in toto* may seem a big price to pay. The real sticking point here for most people is that they fear God. They do not really believe that He is a God of love at all, or turning one's life over to Him would be blessed relief, and there would be no fear in it.

The point of this act of turning one's life over to God is that He will not violate the free will He has given us. And He cannot possibly lead someone who purports to be willing to obey Him one moment and like a balky mule, insists on his own way the next.

DREAM BIG

*He who has, to him shall more be given
and richly given, but whoever has not, from him
shall be taken away even what he has.*

MATTHEW 13:12, MOFFATT

ust one hint about dreams that come true. If they come from God they'll be *big* dreams. For the Creator of our universe can no more be petty than the sun can limit itself to a driblet of shining. In order to get God's help, we have to take the shackles off our spirits, let them stretch and go free. We have to take the blinders off our eyes. We have to scrape the barnacles of prejudices and worn-out ideas from our minds. For the sky is the limit. All the resources of the universe leap to the help of those who dare to dream big.

We might think it would be the opposite. We might think that if we would only ask God for something modest, that would please Him. I only know that's not the way it works.

BLESSINGS DEEP AND WIDE

He will love you and bless you and multiply you.

DEUTERONOMY 7:13

Christianity acknowledges material things and seeks to lift them to serve man's spirit and God's purposes. Our Bible makes no distinction between the secular and the sacred; the everyday and the religious. All of life, every vocational profession, is to be sanctified. Our Bible has a very great deal to say about money, more than most of us want to hear. It takes squarely into account our need of daily bread, of clothes, even our need of beauty. It never ignores sex, in fact looks squarely at it, with neither sentimentality nor whitewash. And so on down all the list of what we call materialism. So that the scope of God's will and His blessing is much wider and deeper and higher than most of us know.

KEEP SHORT ACCOUNTS

In the fear of the LORD there is strong confidence,
and His children will have a place of refuge.

PROVERBS 14:26

f we don't keep our window panes clean," a Bible teacher once said, "the excitement that we feel when we first enter the Christian life will fade." Even an accumulation of small sins can make life seem like a bottle of ginger ale from which all the fizz is gone. So here are some hints:

Discouragement about our failures and stumbling is never the way to handle them. In an old book I found this statement, "All discouragement is from the devil."

Some kind of methodical cleaning out at intervals is necessary if we are to have an uninterrupted fellowship with God.

In trying to keep cleaned out, beware of things that you have an instinctive desire to keep hidden—no matter how insignificant these may seem to you.

PRESENT-MOMENT HAPPINESS

Delight yourself also in the LORD,
and He shall give you the desires of your heart.

PSALM 37:4

ressed by throngs of people, Jesus found respite in the home of Mary and Martha and their brother Lazarus in Bethany. Instinctively, Mary knew that the hours with the Master were golden, so she sat at His feet enjoying Him, drinking in the *now* of every moment.

But Martha was fussily concerned about housekeeping chores and food, having everything just right. She got agitated and annoyed at Mary: "Lord, do You not care that my sister has left me to serve alone? Therefore, tell her to help me." But the Lord replied to her, "Martha, Martha, you are worried and troubled about many things. But one thing is needed and Mary has chosen that good part, which will not be taken away from her" (Luke 10:40–42).

Mary's discovery of happiness in the present moment was, as Jesus pointed out, "the good part" that would bring lasting happiness.

WISDOM FOR THE WAY

The foolishness of God is wiser than men,
and the weakness of God is stronger than men.

1 CORINTHIANS 1:25

hrist never intended that His revelations of truth
should end with the first quarter century of the Christian
era. There are untold riches of understanding and grace
He wants to reveal. Even yet in every phase of Christianity,
there is pioneering to be done, experimentation to be made,
truths to be uncovered. And what adventure God's speaking
directly to us brings to life!

If our Christianity is not just lip-service and pretense, if we
really believe that God exists, that He has all wisdom, and that
He loves us and our world, then we'd better get on with the
matter of listening to the wisdom He waits to give us.

PASSIONATE PURPOSE

*I am come that they might have life,
and that they might have it more abundantly.*

JOHN 10:10

*J*esus always approved of people whose action showed passionate purpose. The woman who broke the alabaster flask of ointment on His feet; Zaccheus who risked making a public spectacle of himself by climbing a tree to see Him. In fact, the word "enthusiasm" comes from *entheos:* in God, or to be inspired and possessed by God. . . .

Having flung out into space a cosmos of yet unexplored reaches, and with the planet Earth filled with wonders great and small to enjoy, God means for every one of us to live fully, zestfully. Boredom thus becomes a negation of the very character of God and of Jesus' purpose in breaking into history.

STOP AND ASK FOR HELP

Anyone who refuses to come to God as
a little child will never be allowed into His kingdom.

MARK 10:15, TLB

A little child who has no shyness or hesitation about asking his parents for what he needs is unconsciously revealing his helplessness, along with a normal, right relationship with his father and mother.

In the same way, asking immediately puts us into a right relationship with God. It is acting out the fact that He is the Creator with the riches and resources we need; we are the creatures who need help. A certain amount of pride and self has to be eliminated for us to ask for help—whether of God or even of another human being. How often we are like the motorist who has lost his way. We will go miles off our route rather than stop to ask for the help we need.

AS LITTLE CHILDREN

Whoever receives one little child like this in My name receives Me.

MATTHEW 18:5

watch my grandchild awaken each morning in anticipation of a day for exploring the great, wide world and everything and everybody in it. Like any normal child, she is naturally happy and joyful. She sees the same objects I do, but looks at them through quite different eyes.

Through exposure to her joy, I am reminded of Christ's extraordinary statement, "Except you are converted and become as little children, you will by no means enter the kingdom of heaven" (Mattt. 18:3). Now I begin to understand why Jesus was careful to specify the diminutive "little children." These tiny ones are still fresh from the hand of their Maker. They have not had time to absorb the prejudices, resentment, social distinctions, cruelties, and conflicts we grown-ups mistakenly call "wisdom."

September

God is always far more willing to give us

good things than we are anxious to have them.

BE HONEST WITH GOD

Draw near to God,
and He will draw near to you.

JAMES 4:8

Throughout all ages Christians have said that when you do not want to pray is when you need it most. Honesty with God helps even then. Though it may sound awful, I start by telling Him that I don't want to talk to Him, but I ask Him to help me.

When we are most helpless, this is when we are most in line to get the most help in prayer. When we feel self-sufficient and able to handle everything, even though we are coming to God in prayer, we are not in nearly as good a position to get answers as when we are totally helpless and honest before God.

When you are honest with Him, then you can begin to see amazing answers to prayer.

RUNNING IN REBELLION

Out of the heart . . . proceed evil thoughts, . . . pride, foolishness.
All these evil things come from within and defile a man.

MARK 7:23

nger in the heart and the contempt of one human being for another precedes the act of murder. Lust in the heart precedes the act of adultery. The last thing God wants for us is conflicts and neuroses that tear us apart. His primary concern is the healthy integration of our heart and will. This health He measures by whether we are still running from Him in rebellion, or are reunited with Him, having found our way back to our heart's home.

The closer I look into the dilemma of our rebellion, the more this central truth stands out for me: behind all broken human relationships lies a basic break—between God and us. We do not often recognize this, being inclined to blame any dislocation in our lives on other people, or on circumstances, and to look for the remedy anywhere but in a reconciliation with God.

THE GOOD-NEWS PRAYER

I know that whatever You ask of God,
God will give You.

JOHN 11:22

Not all our human wants are genuine needs. Moreover, we are often so selfish and short-sighted that the granting of some wants would not be good for us. But Scripture invites us to talk over all our dreams and desires with our Father, then leave what would be best to Him with His wisdom and foreknowledge and loving concern for us.

It is at this point that the Good-News Prayer can be of immense help to all of us. In prayer we dare to walk into the King's presence and present a request that, on the surface, may seem to be trivial or what we would call materialistic. But we add—and mean it—"Lord, You left us that great promise that You can make 'all things work together for good' (Rom. 8:28). So I want You to grant my request only if You can make circumstances intermesh so that this would be good news for everybody involved."

THE TEST OF CHARACTER

If God is for us, who can be against us?

ROMANS 8:31

The Old Testament story of Joseph illustrates perfectly how God can operate in and around and in spite of the sins and shortcomings of men. When Joseph was a seventeen-year-old boy, he was literally at the bottom of a pit. He had been thrown there by his own brothers. Their act was the climax of years of hostility arising out of envy. . . .

The final testing of Joseph's character came many years later when his brothers came from the land of Canaan and stood before him in Egypt, begging to buy grain. They could not possibly have recognized the strong-jawed, bronzed Egyptian as their kinsman.

But the fires of despair had done their work well. Joseph had no thought of vengeance. When he finally revealed his identity, it was in words that could only have been spoken by one whose eyes had so often been washed with tears that now they saw clearly. "But as for you, you thought evil against me; but God meant it unto good. . . ."

LITTLE LAMBS

Train up a child in the way he should go,
and when he is old he will not depart from it.

PROVERBS 22:6

We parents cannot fool our children. Honesty breeds honesty. When we are willing to confess our faults and say to our children, "Forgive me, I lost my temper," or "You know, that was thoughtless and selfish of me. I'm sorry"—we find our children taking a new look at us and at themselves. This kind of give-and-take helps young people form more honest relationships all down the line.

Jesus told us, "Feed my lambs." This means that we are under orders from Him to give our children the best that we know of His love and understanding.

MOVE FORWARD IN FAITH

It is God who arms me with strength,
and makes my way perfect.

PSALM 18:32

As we learn to obey God, the Voice of the Holy Spirit becomes clearer, the instructions more definite. Perhaps another way of saying this is that, as in anything else, we learn through practice.

God's leading must of necessity include the closing of some doors in order that the right door may be opened wide. At the time, it isn't any fun to have a door shut in one's face. But the open door always follows.

When you feel a strong inner check about something, don't move on it. Or to put it positively, always move forward in faith; not out of fear.

Watch the timing on guidance. If a strong inner suggestion is from God, it will strengthen with the passing of time. If not from Him, in a few days or weeks it will probably just evaporate.

THE FAMILY UNIT

I bow my knees to the Father of our Lord Jesus Christ,
from whom the whole family in heaven and earth is named.

EPHESIANS 3:14–15

The family unit is God's first proving ground, the school where He wants to demonstrate the riches He can pour into our lives and how His laws work in everyday life. He will use the very problems we face in the family as the exact vitamins necessary for our growth into mature spirits.

He never said this process would be easy. Never at any point did Jesus promise His followers a bed of rose petals. In fact, He promised the precise opposite. He said that following Him would divide people, often even families.

But the work He has begin in us He is not about to let go unfinished. He always completes what He begins. So if we have started on His road at all, it is pointless to drag our feet and hold back. Here or in the next life, He will see to it that we grow "up in Him."

It Is Finished

He was wounded for our transgressions,
He was bruised for our iniquities.

Isaiah 53:5–7

dam and Eve were not content to be creatures whose only task was to open their hearts and hands to accept and enjoy a veritable rain of gifts and joy and blessings. It was only after they had agreed with the serpent's temptation that surely they "deserved" more, . . . that they first experienced the compulsion to labor.

From that time onward, we have found ourselves caught in the same prison-house of self-effort. We struggle and labor, bearing mighty burdens of tension and worry with uncertain to poor results, until . . . we meet God in the cool of the evening. The unspoken longing in our hearts draws us to Him. We hear ourselves questioning whether there isn't a better way to live, whether we can get back into Eden.

"There's only one way," He tells us. "You have to cease your self-effort and your labor. The work is already finished. Your part is simply to accept it."

TENSION FOR A TIME

To him who overcomes
I will give to eat from the tree of life.

REVELATION 2:7

My experience has been that it is only out of a state of tension that growth can come. We can be too peaceful, I think. We can be so peaceful that the edge if gone off living; that we hear no birdsong; shed no tears; forget the rough edge of pain; no longer know how to laugh.

It is a strange paradox that we have to be willing to suffer the tension for a time, knowing that it is the bridge to the next step in our lives. If we can manage to thank God for it—then we shall find even the tension a blessing.

MAXIMUM SPIRITUAL POWER

The humble also shall increase their joy in the LORD.

ISAIAH 29:19

When I saw the Sistine Chapel in Rome for the first time, I was intrigued to learn something of the working habits of Michelangelo Buonarroti. The four years that it took the great Florentine to paint the vault of the chapel were largely spent in isolation behind locked doors. While very young, Michelangelo had found that for him, work of integrity was impossible without secrecy. . . .

Christ acted on this principle Himself. On one occasion when He had just healed a leper we are told that "Jesus sent him away . . . with the strict injunction, 'Mind you say nothing at all to anybody'" (Matt. 8:4, PHILLIPS).

In the Sermon on the Mount Jesus told us that one condition for maximum spiritual power is secrecy. "When you do a charitable deed, do not let your left hand know what your right hand is doing, that your charitable deed may be in secret; and your Father who sees in secret will Himself reward you openly" (Matt. 6:3–4).

THE CLAIMING PRAYER

I love those who love me, and those
who seek me diligently will find me.

PROVERBS 8:17

God means that all lives be lived in cooperation with Him. His friendship, His plans for us, His riches are awaiting each of us, provided we want Him in our lives. But the riches of His grace must be claimed. "You have not, because you ask not" (James 4:2).

The process goes like this:

- God has made a promise.
- If there are conditions attached to it, we do our best to meet them.
- We make an act at a specific time and place of claiming this promise.
- God fulfills the promise in His own time and way.

LIGHT ON OUR PATH

I will strengthen them in the LORD,
and they shall walk up and down in His name.

ZECHARIAH 10:12

From my own experience and that of many others, I know that the Spirit's guidance is just as real in our century as it was in the days when He guided the apostles.

The Spirit cannot guide us, however, if we insist on finding our own way. It is as if we, groping along in the dark, are offered a powerful lantern to light our path, but refuse it, preferring to stumble along striking one flickering match after the other.

Instead, first we have to ask the Spirit to lead us. Then by an act of will place our life situations and our future in His hands; and then trust that He will get His instructions through to us.

PLAIN GOODWILL

*I will heal them and reveal to
them the abundance of peace and truth.*

JEREMIAH 33:6

ecently I have been pondering the principle of
the power of joy in relation to world peace. Even
for those who completely believe in prayer, it isn't
easy to know how to pray for other nations. It's especially hard
when their ideals are not ours, and when we are considered
enemies.

But perhaps Christ is saying to us: "The people of all nations
are My children. If you are going to be true sons of My Father,
you are going to have to bless those who curse you, even pray
for those who spitefully use you."

Now obviously we cannot bless and pray for people who
spitefully use us, or with whom we are at odds, unless our
prayer has that element of just plain goodwill that lies at the
heart of joy and love.

CLAIMING GOD'S PROMISES

*His divine power has given to us
all things that pertain to life and godliness.*

2 PETER 1:3

noticed a strange sentence written on the flyleaf of Peter Marshall's Bible:

*It is the word of a Gentleman of the most
strict and sacred honor, so there's an end of it.*
—David Livingston

Underneath the inscription, Peter had signed his own name.

When I asked Peter for an explanation of the words, he thumped the cover of his Bible and said, "In these pages are the living words of the living God. These words include a lot of promises, many of them with conditions attached. But they weren't meant just for the Israelites. They were meant for us too. All we have to do is to meet the conditions, then step up and claim them."

GETTING ALONG

*"I will be a Father to you, and you shall
be My sons and daughters," says the Lord Almighty*

2 CORINTHIANS 6:18

The family is meant to be the training ground for life—a true microcosm of the world outside the home. My experience would indicate that the Lord is primarily interested in our growing up into the stature of mature personalities. Naturally, He wants us to be happy. Of course, He wants us to have fun. But some of us have discovered that hard way that happiness never comes as an end in itself, always a dividend. And it does not take much of a look around today's world to pinpoint the chief block to maturity: person getting along with person.

So how does one learn to get along with others? By living elbow to elbow in a family situation where varying interests and personalities whittle away at selfishness, sandpaper the sharp edges of impatience, and bend us into flexibility.

LEAVE THE RESULTS TO HIM

Show me Your ways, O LORD;
teach me Your paths.

PSALM 25:4

Often we miss the wisdom He seeks to give us because we are so intent on the high-flown super-spirituality of our preconceived image of Christ.

Through all of this we need to be careful not to confuse what the old egocentric self wants—to succeed, to get well, to be loved—with that positive, trusting, obedient attitude that wants only God's will for us. . . .

Self-will turns the eyes on self and what self strongly wants.

Faith turns the eyes on Christ to ask Him what He wants.

Self-will worries about the results.

Faith worries only about obedience, then leaves the result to Jesus.

PERSONAL PROMISES

*The hand of our God is upon
all those for good who seek Him.*

EZRA 8:22

he promises that follow are a part of the fabric of my life. Each of them represents a milestone in my personal history. I share them with you as the gold they are.

When I need physical strength and good health—If the Spirit of Him who raised Jesus from the dead dwells in you, He . . . will also give life to your mortal bodies through His Spirit who dwells in you (Rom. 8:11).

When I need material help—If God so clothes the grass of the field . . . will He not much more clothe you, O you of little faith? (Matt. 6:30)

When I wonder if God understands what I'm up against—But Jesus the Son of God is our great High Priest who has gone to heaven itself to help us; therefore let us never stop trusting Him. This High Priest of ours understands our weakness since he had the same temptations we do, though he never once gave way to them and sinned (Heb. 4:14–15, TLB).

RESTORATION

I will restore to you the years that the swarming locust has eaten. . . .
You shall . . . praise the name of the LORD your God.

JOEL 2:25–26

Almost every mail brings letters from people grieving over a mistake made earlier in life—selecting the wrong mate for marriage, for example, or some sin that has scarred their lives. . . . Is there, people are asking, any way back? Indeed there is! . . . .

Our part in this restoration is to look squarely at the place where we got off the track and have the courage not to minimize our sin or to blame it on anybody but ourselves.

The reason we mustn't underplay wrongdoing is that the price of setting it right came high—even to God Himself. He could not have made those promises of forgiveness and restoration . . . , had He not known that at a given point in history, Christ Jesus would die on a wooden gibbet on a hill outside Jerusalem and by the shedding of His blood, make possible the Father's forgiveness of you and me—past, present, and future.

THE SOURCE OF SUPPLY

But my God shall supply all your need
according to His riches in glory by Christ Jesus.

PHILIPPIANS 4:19

As long as we have a low threshold of expectation limited to our needs and those of our immediate family, we probably won't turn to God for help. . . . But when we, in obedience to God, decide to be totally His person at His disposal and take on some enormous task He requires of us, then we are going to find ourselves thrown upon His unlimited supply.

How God supplies is spelled out for us in Scripture.

The first step is to get our eyes off our own need, to look instead at God's unlimited supply. One of Christ's fundamental premises was that God the Father controls all of earth's material resources. Simple words, but what a tremendous assertion.

Since we are His children and all the world's riches belong to the King, it follows that He can and will take care of our physical needs.

GIVE—AND GET ABUNDANCE

Give, and it will be given to you: good measure,
pressed down, shaken together, and running over
will be put into your bosom.

LUKE 6:38

To receive, one must give, even out of poverty. This is not only a promise, but a fact of the Father's world, part of the rhythm of the universe. In the last century every farmer knew it as he primed the pump by pouring the bucket of water in to start the water flowing. We feel it each time we stand on an ocean beach and feel the tugging rhythm of the tide washing the sand beneath our feet. We experience it when we step out on God's promise and to our astonishment discover that our Father will never allow Himself to be in debt to any child of His.

Here is an exciting principle for all those in life's holes. Of what do we have a shortage? Money? Household possessions? Ideas? Friends? Love? Prayer-power? Creativity? Strength? Health? Whatever it is, when we, under God's direction, give away out of our shortage, like the tide returning we get back abundance—"good measure, pressed down, running over."

CREATIVE IN CHRIST

*God . . . does great things
which we cannot comprehend.*

JOB 37:5

The essence of creativity is to seek God first, making full use of whatever talent is yours—to give priority to the Kingdom of God and His righteousness. Then as we begin living in the Kingdom of God on earth, He will show us how to make the best use of our talents. We begin with a seed idea or a seed talent and create something that other people need or enjoy. That plunges us directly into the stream of the Creator's unending creativity and generosity.

THE COINAGE OF CHRIST'S KINGDOM

Oh, taste and see that the LORD is good;
blessed is the man who trusts in Him!

PSALM 34:8

Nowhere in Scripture can I find any justification for the idea that prayer should be limited to spiritual needs. So far as I can understand, Jesus taught us quite the opposite.

It is as if God, knowing full well that while we are in these bodies of flesh and blood are going to be physical creatures of this earth, says to us, "There's only one place and one way you can learn of Me, that's just as you are in your present circumstances. Let's deal with your obvious needs and lacks by looking at your assets—no matter how small. I'll show you step by step how to approach Me, how the coinage of My kingdom is put into circulation, how to hand Me your lack and get back My adequacy. What better demonstration of My reality and My love and caring for you could you have? Come, try it."

Taste and see that the Lord is good. Prove Him!

GOD CHANGES HEARTS

*Through the LORD's mercies we are
not consumed, because His compassions fail not.*

LAMENTATIONS 3:22

*J*esus chose God's way, not man's, to deal with the iniquity He loathed. Judas Iscariot wanted his Master to use the world's technique by rebelling against Rome. Judas, the classic revolutionary, wanted armed political rebellion against the godless forces of Rome. Jesus deliberately refused, thereby telling us for all time, "No, the end does *not* justify the means." He chose instead God's way of changing men's hearts and minds and lives via the Cross.

Certainly we cannot "love righteousness" and "hate iniquity," then use any of iniquity's techniques. Those who recognize in Jesus of Nazareth the First Rebel, see equally that His weapons were never those of unrighteousness. He will never allow us to do evil with the claim that it's to achieve justice or right.

QUIT COMPLAINING

I will dwell in them and walk among them.
I will be their God, and they shall be My people.

2 CORINTHIANS 6:16

From the time the Chosen People first left Egypt, God had been trying to teach them some facts about Himself: first, He was (and is) a personal God. . . . As a Father, no detail of His children's lives was beneath His notice—from the dimensions of the wilderness tabernacle or the tassels on the hem of the priests' robes, to the adjudication of the minutest quarrel between neighbors.

It follows that when the Israelites or any of us have really accepted God as our Father in the personal way He means it, then we are going to trust the circumstances He permits us to have. That is why our grumbling about God's provision is at the least attributing more power to circumstances and to evil than to God. And murmuring and rebellion can lose us our personal Promised Land. Our Promised Land means God's will perfectly done in our life and affairs . . . . But we can miss all of it through complaining.

GOD GIVES VICTORY

The Lord knows how to
deliver the godly out of temptations.

2 PETER 2:9

Very often, when life has handed us some injustice or when we have stuck faithfully through some protracted trial, we think we deserve a "little fun" by a fling into sinning. A degree of self-pity joins the blown-up pride of our self-congratulation at having been so patient and reliable. Many of us have found out to our sorrow what a deadly brew this is. Our eyes are completely off Christ and on ourselves. Out of this little mess Satan has worked some great triumphs.

But what if we are already in the middle of such a mess? What if one's life is snarled up by habit-patterns, bad human relationships, fears that one can't get rid of, debts, and illness? What then? Is there any hope?

There certainly is! That's precisely the good news Christ brings us. . . : "Behold, I give you the authority . . . over all the power of the enemy; and nothing shall by any means hurt you" (Luke 10:19).

WALKING IN THE LIGHT

Walk as children of light . . .
finding out what is acceptable to the Lord.

EPHESIANS 5:8–10)

We walk as children of light when we insist upon transparent openness and honesty, no dark secrets, no duplicity, lies, or double-dealing. . . . Hidden sin—no matter how carefully denied, glossed over, and secreted away—will give Satan his beachhead and result in our inability to stand victoriously before the enemy or any of his cohorts. The emphasis here is on any accursed thing being tucked back in our lives, hidden out of sight. We may have almost forgotten about it, but Satan never forgets. For us, the result will be failure every time. This is the reason that Jesus had so much to say about the necessity of light and our coming to the light. When men's deeds are evil, they love darkness rather than light.

So it helps to stay aware of this principle: whenever we prefer to keep something secret or hidden, tucked away in the darkness, we do well to question our real motives.

GOD OF THE SUPERNATURAL

O LORD my God, You are very great:
You are clothed with honor and majesty.

PSALM 104:1

The antidote to negativism is the power of God. It is a transforming power in and over the world He has made. On the reality of that power Scripture never backs down or gives ground. From the time God called Moses to lead His people, through the plagues visited on the Egyptians, through the parting of the Red Sea, through many miracles in the desert, God was saying, "I do have power. I am the God of the supernatural. You are to trust Me for more than you would expect through 'natural' law or 'natural' causation."

Power over what? Precisely those factors about which the Israelites murmured—the harsh desert, the difficulties of their trek, physical ailments and illnesses, and the hostility of their enemies. In other words, over the external conditions of life.

BLESSED ASSURANCE

Blessed are the pure in heart,
for they shall see God.

MATTHEW 5:8

In my battle to stop using sleeping pills each
night, when I stopped rebelling and sought God
even at the point of sleeplessness, then I was given the
praise-filled message of the old hymn:

> *Blessed assurance, Jesus is mine! . . . .*
> *This is my story, this is my song,*
> *Praising my Savior all the day long.*

In retrospect I could see the steps—from rebellion, to
acceptance, to praise, to God changing the situation. I began to
see more clearly, too, why God sets Himself so seriously against
a disobedient or rebellious or judgmental spirit: this is the precise
frame of heart and mind that blocks His loving intervention
on our behalf.

ONE HEART

I will give them one heart,
and I will put a new spirit within them . . . that they
may walk in My statutes and keep My judgments.

EZEKIEL 11:19–20

What would be the difference in our world today if we began to let the Cross work its change in our hearts? . . .

Rebellion and mutiny would be seen as a paltry playing at life as we enter into the glorious liberty of the children of God. What that liberty could mean for us was spelled out long ago at the beginning of God's dealings with the Israelites. It is a vision that has haunted us ever since. . .

The good earth, its seas, lakes, rivers, and streams, the air, the trees, the animals, will no longer be ravaged by man. Crops would be blessed and sufficient to end hunger for all mankind. The nation that produces plenty would rush its aid and know-how to those countries with less.

Marriage and family life would thrive and be blessed. Once again babies would be wanted and cherished.

THE NAME(S) OF JESUS

Not unto us, O LORD, not unto us,
but to Your name give glory.

PSALM 115:1

There is great significance in the many names Scripture gives to Jesus Christ, among them:

The Last Adam	Light of the World	Saviour
Bread of Life	The Good Shepherd	Cornerstone
The Door	Counselor	King of Kings
The Prince of Peace	The Lamb of God	Great High Priest

When we think of Jesus' ringing statement after His resurrection, "All power is given unto me in heaven and in earth . . . (Matt. 28:18), we see why many descriptive words are needed to cover "all power." But all of them are caught up and comprehended in the name of Jesus. Again and again we are assured that the power to save, to redeem, to heal, to guide, to give wisdom, to protect, is wrapped up and focused like a laser beam in this "Name."

October

All of God's good gifts

are given by pure grace.

GETTING RID OF FEAR

You did not receive the spirit of bondage again to fear,
but you received the Spirit of adoption by whom we cry out, "Abba Father."

ROMANS 8:15

Any emotion or attitude that disorients or disintegrates human personality so that we miss the mark is certainly a sin—a negative to be gotten rid of. Whether at its simplest level when fear "roots us to the spot" or causes our knees to buckle, or a more sophisticated form of jealousy—fear, or the fear of hardship or disaster in times of economic depression—it destroys coordination, riddles personality, blocks logical thinking, and makes creative solutions to problems impossible.

By worrying and fretting, we are really saying, "I don't believe God can help me, and I do not trust Him." Thereby we are sinning against God by impugning His character and calling Him a liar.

At that point there is only one way to get rid of fear; like any sin, we must recognize it, confess it in true repentance, claim God's sure promise of forgiveness, . . . rise and get on with life.

GIVING TO GOD

The LORD is my shepherd; I shall not want.

PSALM 23:1

Tithing was a practice God asked of the Jewish people back in Old Testament times. It means giving to God through giving to others a minimum of one-tenth of one's gross income or harvest or cattle production or whatever. "Minimum" because even as Christ upholds tithing, He also strengthens it by often asking that we give away more than the base ten percent.

In teaching the practice of tithing to the Jews, God was seeing to it that they would have an unending demonstration of how sound the coin of His kingdom is. To buttress this further He gave them—and us—that magnificent promise: "Bring all the tithes into the storehouse, that there may be food in My house, and try Me now in this," says the LORD of hosts, "If I will not open for you the windows of heaven and pour out for you such blessing, that there will not be room enough to receive it" (Mal. 3:10).

When we put God first, we won't have to worry about our supply.

GETTING TO KNOW GOD

Show me Your ways, O LORD; teach me Your paths.
Lead me in Your truth and teach me.

PSALM 25:4

*I*n order to grow in the faith and become a mature Christian, you have to have spiritual food. It's a process of education, of getting to know this God to whom you have given your life.

Thus getting on with the kingdom of God necessarily means total involvement for each of us.

At such a time we have a basic choice to make about our reading. . . . Shall we center on "escape literature" or "involvement literature"? We need to be thoughtful about the choice. For escape literature can contribute nothing, lead nowhere except to stagnation. Involvement literature, on the other hand, takes us directly to that table so richly laden with spiritual food, where the Lord Himself is Host.

We must know what we believe and why we believe it.

GRACIOUS TRAITS

If we live in the Spirit,
let us also walk in the Spirit.

GALATIANS 5:25

Once we have been born again and have received the Holy Spirit, we experience a newness of life with many changes. Some involve deep and extensive inner transformation. Study the fifth chapter of Galatians and note the element of change that Paul depicts and his list of high character traits that should be common to all who receive the Spirit: love, a great joy and gladness, an even temper and patience, kindness and generosity in our judgment of our fellows, faithfulness (hanging in there), gentleness, self-control and self-restraint.

When we allow the Spirit to develop in us these gracious traits, then, like the boy Jesus growing up, we, too, will "increase in wisdom . . . and in favor with God and man."

OUR GREATEST WEAPON

Your word I have hidden in my heart,
that I might not sin against You.

PSALM 119:11

One of our greatest weapons against the Destroyer is the use of Scripture as truth wielded as the "sword of the Spirit." Jesus' repeated use of "It is written" in His wilderness temptations is a vivid example. Of course, in order to use Scripture in this way, we have to get into the habit of reading it so that the truth cast in the cadences of the great English of the Bible sinks deeply into heart and mind. I have found that when I do my part, the Holy Spirit can do His. So often it has happened! It is as if the Helper searches through the library stacks of my unconscious where all manner of information has been filed away (much of it long since forgotten by the conscious mind) and produces the particular "It is written" needed for the moment of battle.

Always Satan flees before this.

FAITHLESS FEAR

He delivers and rescues, and He works
signs and wonders in heaven and on earth.

DANIEL 6:27

As Jesus walked the earth and so frequently felt fear in those around Him, again and again we hear that cry of His, "O men, how little you trust Him!" In the cry there was more than a little rebuke and sorrow along with a sort of marveling astonishment that men could be so blind: "Why are you afraid? How little you trust God!" (Matt. 8:21)

Behind Jesus' sharp reaction to our faithless fears lay His consistent viewpoint that this is our Father's world, still in His control. Nor did Jesus ever use the word "Father" lightly out of slick sentimentality. He taught that God deals with each of us personally in the way the best of fathers would. Therefore, the kind of love necessary to bring His kingdom on earth is not brotherly love, but fatherly love. When we take Jesus' teachings (for example, the last four Beatitudes) in the light of this fatherly love, what has before seemed hopelessly idealistic becomes practical and possible.

THE ARMOR OF LIGHT

Let us cast off the works of darkness,
and let us put on the armor of light.

ROMANS 13:12

In other places in the Bible the pieces of our armor are described. Integrity is our coat of mail, truth is our belt, salvation is our helmet. Our shoes are the stability of the gospel of peace. And above all, faith is our shield.

This kind of armor suggests that every hour of every day we are in the thick of battle. Not only must we put on that armor of light, but we must practice walking in it on ordinary days when we think we feel no danger. . . . We are putting on the coat of mail when we resolutely expel dishonesty from our lives. We are sharpening our spiritual sword as we memorize some of the great passages of Scripture and seek out the life-giving promises.

THE DIVINE GUEST

When He, the Spirit of truth,
has come, He will guide you into all truth.

JOHN 16:13

It is plain from Scripture that we can't possibly enter into a new life in Christ or be a child of God at all without knowing the Spirit. However, there is a big difference between being indwelt by the Spirit and being "filled" with His presence. For years (sometimes a lifetime) a Christian can keep the Spirit at a sub-basement level by insisting on running his own life. Then through teaching or need—or both—the person consciously recognizes the divine Guest's presence, and opens the hitherto closed doors into certain rooms in his being so that the Spirit can enter there too. Thus the individual now deliberately abandons himself to the Helper's control.

WILLING TO ACCEPT GOD'S WILL

He who has begun a good work in you
will complete it until the day of Jesus Christ.

PHILIPPIANS 1:6

God is intent on our learning how to obey Him in the totality of life. Back in 1943–1944 my personal desire for health was the focal point of reality for me. Perhaps so much of me had been packed into that eager longing that there was no room for God to enter and do anything at all so long as my myopic thinking was equating "life" with the health I wanted.

Everything turns here on what constitutes life. In the end God's answer was infinitely more inclusive and richer than mine. So long as I was assuming that fullness of life corresponded to what I was striving for, I was actually deifying my own goal. And "Thou shalt have no other gods before Me" had to apply to my personal desires. There was nothing for it but to "put away" that most beloved of all idols inscribed "What I want." The scrapping of a treasure is always painful.

OUR MAGNIFICENT MAKER

The earth is the LORD's, and all its fullness,
the world and those who dwell therein.

PSALM 24:1

To call our Father in heaven a King, in my opinion, is to understate the truth. Consider the prodigality of the Father's world. He did not create a single kind of fern, but some 10,000 kinds; not one type of palm tree, but 1500 different palms. Not one insect, but 625,000 and more that scientists have not yet named. Astronomers now estimate that there are a hundred billion galaxies of stars in the universe, of which earth's Milky Way is but one: There are a million galaxies inside the bowl of the Big Dipper alone. No poverty complex in the Creator of such infinitude!

THE HELPER

By this we know that He abides in us,
by the Spirit whom He has given us.

1 JOHN 3:24

You and I are living in rough times. We must make our way through minefields of evil, booby traps of deception, brush fires of sickness and disease, wastelands of economic disaster, burning deserts of disappointment. "I won't take you out of this world," Jesus told us. "But don't be afraid, because I've overcome that world of dangers. All power is Mine. I promise to be with you always."

"How, Lord? How are you with us?"

"Through the Helper."

It is true. He is here. We who in moments of desperation have asked, "What can I do? What is there left?" have felt His answering presence and experienced His help. . . . We know now . . . that He always holds out to us the exciting promise of something more.

TOO GLORIOUS!

How precious also are Your thoughts
to me, O God! How great is the sum of them!

PSALM 139:17

In Psalm 139 God's plan for each life is pictured as a path from which man strays. But our God knows all about our wanderings off His path. Not only that, His Presence goes behind us as well as before:

"O Lord, You have examined my heart and know everything about me. You know when I sit or stand. . . . Every moment You know where I am. . . . You both precede and follow me, and place Your hand of blessing on my head. This is too glorious, too wonderful to believe! I can *never* be lost to Your Spirit!" (Psalm 139:1–7 TLB)

Most of us believe that God can handle the "befores" provided we cooperate; but that He can also walk into our past and correct our mistakes, that seems too good to be true.

WISDOM OR WILLFULNESS?

He will teach us His ways, and we shall walk in His paths.

ISAIAH 2:3

The temptation to hang onto self-will is tagged "man's autonomy" and the bait is our covetousness for understanding. It's a temptation to which I, for one, have succumbed as often as most people by always wanting to know "Why?" I've even handed myself accolades for that. Doesn't that show that I'm a seeker, even a spiritual researcher? Didn't even Solomon ask for the gift of wisdom?

No, it doesn't prove much of anything except that I'm like my Mother Eve. She could have offered up the same rationalizations . . . "And when the woman saw that it was a tree to be desired to make one *wise*. . . she . . . did eat."

Wisdom . . . understanding—all tempting bait. Except for the thoughts God chooses to share with us, it's still forbidden fruit. So long as we wear the garment of flesh, we can never understand the mind of our Creator.

THE SET OF OUR WILL

I pray that your love may abound still
more and more in knowledge and all discernment.

PHILIPPIANS 1:9

We petition, we pray, we wait, but we do not "feel" any different. Feelings are at the bottom of most of our Christian difficulties. Our emotions are often painfully misleading, and at best we have imperfect control over them. . . . Our feelings can be affected by such irrelevant matters as the mood of those around us, by whether we had a good night's sleep. . . .

What is the remedy? It is simplicity itself: our emotions are not the real us. The motivating force at the center of our physical being is our will. . . . The will is the governing power in us, the rudder, the spring of all our actions. Before God we are responsible only for the set of that will—whether we decide for God's will or insist on self-will.

OPEN HANDS, OPEN HEARTS

Bearing with one another, and forgiving one another, . . .
even as Christ forgave you, so you also must do.

COLOSSIANS 3:13

*L*et's consider the matter of resentments. Jesus
Christ was devastating in what He had to say
about unforgiven hurts and wrongs. . . .

The secret is to pray something like this: "*Lord, You have
plainly told me that all vengeance is Yours, not my business at all, and
that I must forgive. I am willing to forgive, but I've tried over and over,
and the surging resentments keep coming back. In my will I hand this
bitterness over to You. Here I hold it out to You in my open hand. I promise
only that I will not again close my fist and reclaim the resentment. Now I
ask You to take it and handle these emotions that I cannot handle.*"

There one leaves the matter. When the thoughts return to it,
there is the quiet inner assertion that it has been turned over to
God, and that He is taking care of it. Always for me, in a matter
of hours or days, I find the resentment evaporates and in its
place—peace.

PRESUMPTION OR FAITH?

This is the victory that has overcome the world—our faith.

1 JOHN 5:4

How can we tell the difference between presumption and faith? Presumption assumes something to be true in the absence of God's proof to the contrary. Faith hears and receives God's word firsthand via the Spirit speaking to our spirit, and moves forward only on that word.

Jesus meant it when He said, "The Son . . . does only what He sees the Father doing." Notice the word *only* in Jesus' statement. That's altogether different from doing something because God hasn't said *not* to do it. The latter road is a tangled maze of errors, mapped out by Satan. When we run out ahead of God, an element of daring God and of boldness bordering on impertinence, even unbelief, enters the situation.

But when we *have* gotten His directives and obeyed them, we no longer have to carry the responsibility for the results. Jesus is the Healer. The results are His.

THE FATHERLINESS OF GOD

You, O LORD, are our Father;
our Redeemer from Everlasting is Your name.

ISAIAH 63:16

Whether small children or grown-up children, we need to develop a sense of dependence on the Fatherliness of God. It may seem to us at first thought that any dependence is the opposite of strength or a mature personality. But when we look closely at Jesus, we see that this is not so. Always the Master gave the impression of a moment-by-moment companionship and dialogue with the Father, yet here was a Man afraid of nothing. Not fearing men's opinions of Him, He spoke the truth bluntly. He was not afraid of unpopularity because He knew that when we are true to our real self, it is impossible to please everyone. He did not cringe when He walked through the mob at Nazareth. Here was a truly dangerous mob-lynching scene. Yet with Jesus' faith in the Father, He strode through the midst of them with such assurance that the crowd simply faded before Him.

LIFE MUST GO ON

I will heal them and reveal to them
the abundance of peace and truth.

JEREMIAH 33:6

t takes most of us a long time to face up to the fact that not all the grieving in the world will bring the one we love back to our side; that life must go on.

So if you are one of those who is ready to face the challenge and the joy of a new life, this is what you do: Recognize that sorrow is an emotion, and that you have little control over it. You know that God loves your loved one who is now with Him, and that He loves you. God does have a present plan for your life. So take firm grip on your will. That's what God has been waiting for. Tell Him that you *will* be happy again, that you hand the grief over to Him, even as you have handed resentment and lack of faith. Ask Him to do what you cannot do—take away the raw and harrowing emotion and put in its place the peace and joy He came to earth to give. There you leave it.

And it works. Always it works.

EVERY NEED SUPPLIED

My help comes from the LORD,
who made heaven and earth.

PSALM 121:2

George Müeller, who opened one of the first orphanages in England, was that rare combination: a business-minded man, as well as a Christian who habitually kept careful records of everything—even answers to prayer.

Muller became so convinced of God's trustworthiness in practical matters that he closed one door after another behind him in order to prove this to the world. First, he refused any regular salary. Then he literally sold all that he had, even his household goods, and gave all to the poor. In this his courageous wife concurred. The point of this stripping of self was that he wished to leave himself no material crutch; his every need would have to be supplied by God . . . as indeed it was.

MAKE UP YOUR MIND

He who heeds the word wisely will find good,
and whoever trusts in the LORD, happy is he.

PROVERBS 16:20

As we see our situation through God's eyes we begin to understand how intensely practical He is in dealing with us, His finite creatures.

Reflecting that practicality, Jesus' directives to us are always specific, never vague and generalized. He would not allow those who came running after Him wailing, "Lord, have mercy," to stop there; He was forever forcing them out of this "general blessing" area by asking questions like "What do you want Me to do for you?" In other words, "Use your mind, my son. Make up your heart. God is not the Father of sloppy thinking. Nor is He the Lord of generalizing."

At first glance it may seem odd that the more extensive our need, the more important it is to get God's guidance on pinpointing where and how He wants His supply to come to us. It's as if once we find the first right thread to pull, the whole of our tangled problem begins to unravel.

FEARFUL FANTASIES

Blessed be the LORD, my Rock, . . .
my high tower and my deliverer.

PSALM 144:1–2

As Jesus a tower-light of protection against fear? Yes, because Jesus is Light and that Light can melt and dispel these submerged incapacitating fantasies. Sometimes it helps to write down one's fears, then hold them up one by one to the light of Christ's clear understanding. Never is Jesus as the Light of the World more clear than in these murky areas of our semi-conscious fears, most of them unreal and psychotic. The trouble with the imaginary fears is that they can, if allowed to go on and on unchallenged, really destroy. As we talk over each fear on the list with Christ, He will illuminate for us some steps to expose them for what they really are. . . .

Not only new confidence but real growth in character follows this facing up to what we fear. Provided we are acting under God's direction.

IN JESUS' NAME

And whatever you ask in My name,
that I will do, that the Father may be glorified in the Son.

JOHN 14:13

When we pray "in Jesus' Name," we are not simply verbalizing a word or a phrase; rather, our petition is to the complete character of the Lord and all of the power implicit in His Name. The Scripture abounds in "holy mysteries" and the full meaning of praying in the Name of Jesus is one of those mysteries. In heaven, the mystery is understood; on earth, we shall probably never know it fully. Yet as we step out in faith using that Name, we do learn bit by bit. Even some of Christ's first followers, the seventy whom He sent out two-by-two during His earthly ministry, discovered early that His Name had power indeed:

> "Then the seventy returned with joy, saying,
> 'Lord, even the demons are subject to us in Your
> name" (Luke 10:17).

THE PROBLEM OF WILL

The Father has not left Me alone,
for I always do those things that please Him.

JOHN 8:29

wanted to look more closely at how Jesus handled the problem of will. I was startled to find that He (before His resurrection and glorification) insisted upon His helplessness:

"The Son can do nothing of Himself, but what He sees the Father do . . ." (John 5:19).

Jesus' helplessness meant a total dependence upon His Father for everything. But His *will*, what of that? Since Jesus' perfect humanity was as real as His divinity, His would have been a strong human will, stronger than any of ours. Over and over He reiterated that He had handed over that will:

"I have come down from heaven, not to do My own will, but the will of Him who sent Me" (John 6:38).

"My food is to do the will of Him who sent Me . . ." (John 4:34).

And at the end, He was "obedient even unto death".

PRESENT IN ALL PLACES

God is Spirit, and those who worship Him
must worship in spirit and truth.

JOHN 4:24

It stretches our minds to grasp the fact of God as Spirit. Perhaps it is because not enough Christians have grasped this, that the omnipresence (present in all places at all time) and the omniscience (having infinite understanding and insight) of God are not credible to the skeptic.

Since the Father is a Spirit, the world around us is filled with His presence. To the extent that we put our egos to death, God as spirit can fill our minds and bodies, and live in us, literally making us new creatures. This is one of the most exciting teachings of the New Testament. Its ramifications can transform every area of life.

HOPE IN OUR HELPLESSNESS

He knows our frame;
He remembers that we are dust.

PSALM 103:14

Helplessness is a terrifying thing to most of us. We resist it, deny it. . . .

But helplessness is actually one of the greatest assets a human being can have. . . . In my case, the most spectacular answers to prayer have come following a period when I could do nothing for myself at all.

The Psalmist says, "When I was hemmed in, thou hast freed me often." Gradually I have come to recognize this hemming-in process as one of God's most loving and effective devices for teaching us that He is gloriously adequate for our problems.

THE RIGHT SOURCE

I believe; help my unbelief.

MARK 9:24

New Testament folks must have been quite like you and me. Clearly we are mirrored in the father who knelt before Christ pleading for his son's deliverance (Mark 9:14–29). This man had experienced no assurance in prayer. He was discouraged. He appealed to the love of God but doubted God's power. Jesus replied sternly and emphatically, "If you can believe, all things are possible to him who believes."

This brought the father, with tears, to a clear admission of his wavering faith and an appeal to Jesus for more faith. The man wasn't perfect; he had doubts and fears just as we have. But he was honest, and he went to the right Source to get his defective faith steadied.

It was enough! His son was cured!

THE FATHER'S DELIGHT

The Son of Man has come to save that which was lost.

MATTHEW 18:11

*J*esus is the portrait of God. Here is the One who leaves the ninety-nine sheep safely in the fold and goes out after the one lost lamb—because He cares. By every word and deed, Jesus made it clear that His Father not only cares, but that no detail of any life is too insignificant for His loving providence.

The accounts of Jesus' miracles portray Him working out His Father's love for each man, each woman, each child. He went about demonstrating the Father's delight in restoring deranged minds to sanity, sight to blind eyes, hearing to deaf ears. . . .

So often the styluses of the Gospel narrators etched the word "compassion." No wonder! In Jesus they had encountered a caring of such depth and magnitude, yet often stooping to attend to such minute detail, that language failed them in describing it. He who was the embodied revelation of God had the profoundest sense of the sacredness of human personality of any man in history.

REJOICE ALWAYS

Rejoice in the Lord always. Again I will say, rejoice!

PHILIPPIANS 4:4

As Paul and Silas, still bruised and bleeding [in prison], turned their minds from self and sang their thanksgiving to the Lord, an earthquake rocked the city of Philippi, shook the foundation of the prison, burst the gates, and wrenched the chains from the walls. Two other miracles followed quickly. The jailer and his entire household became followers of Christ. And when morning dawned the city authorities in a complete about-face withdrew all charges and commanded Paul and Silas to "depart, and go in peace."

As the former prisoners strode on their way, Paul could exult, "I have learned in whatsoever state I am, to be content" (Phil. 4:11).

Out of such a framework, we would do well to listen to this giant among apostles when he admonishes us to "Rejoice in the Lord *always*: and again I say, rejoice . . . in everything by prayer and supplication with thanksgiving let your requests be made known unto God" (Phil. 4:4–6).

PERFECT OBEDIENCE, PERFECT HAPPINESS

Show me Your ways, O LORD;
teach me Your paths.

PSALM 25:4

When Jesus says, "Follow Me," not a one of us is going to drop our fishing nets to leave all and go after Him—unless we feel we can trust Him.

So we're back full circle to the only basis there is for obedience—love and trust. It may seem hard to be asked to have this kind of confidence before we have had personal experiences of God. But He also helps us out of that dilemma. The moment we "purpose in our heart" to obey Him, at that instant He comes to help us. His incomparable gift is the ability to obey, to move out into what usually looks like uncharted and dangerous country.

ENFOLDED IN GOD

Search me, O God, and know my heart; try me,
and know my anxieties; . . . and lead me in the way everlasting.

PSALM 139:23–24

God knows all about each of us, our mistakes and wanderings off the path (Ps. 139:1–4). He has "beset" us (one translation says "enfolds"), "behind and before"(vs. 5). Most of us believe that God can handle the future, the "before," but that God can reach into our past, the "behind," blazes out at us as a new and wonderful truth.

The Psalmist says that we can go nowhere beyond the reach of God's hand (vv. 8–10); and life can never get so black that God cannot lead us and hold us (vv. 10–12).

Our God is the only One Who can take life's rubbish heap—our mistakes, disappointments, disobedience, and sin—and through divine alchemy, make even these "to work together for good." If this were not true, the gospel would be for the angels, not for us imperfect creatures still walking the warm earth.

THE VINE AND THE BRANCHES

Without me, you can do nothing.

JOHN 15:5

*N*othing? That seems a trifle sweeping. Perhaps Jesus meant simply that we shall be more effective with His help than without it.

But when we go back to the context in which the statement is made, we find that Jesus meant precisely what He said. This is the allegory of the vine and the branches: "I am the vine, you are the branches." The point is not that the branches will do better when they are attached to the vine. Unless attached, the branches must wither and die.

November

Talk it over with the Father,

then leave the outcome to His wisdom.

ABUNDANT LIFE

I have come that they may have life,
and that they may have it more abundantly.

JOHN 10:10

Watch Jesus as God in action. He came to earth to destroy the works of the Devil (1 John 3:8). In Christ's eyes the Devil's works were any attitude or deed that degraded or destroyed any part of God's handiwork—sin, disease, demon-possession, death. Jesus saw all these manifestations of evil with a single eye. He was against them!

He never condemned sinners. To condemn or judge was to Him simply a waste of time. He forgave, cleansed, and restored. He never refused to heal anyone who came to Him (Matt. 12:15). . . . He seems to have broken up every funeral He attended (Luke 7:12–16).

What is God's will? As we watch God in action through Jesus only one answer is possible. God's will is always for the creative, the positive, for building up and lifting up.

LEARNING TO WAIT

*It is good that one should hope and
wait quietly for the salvation of the LORD.*

LAMENTATIONS 3:26

Here are some of the scriptural promises for those who learn to wait:

The LORD is good to those who wait for Him . . . (Lam. 3:25).
Those who wait on the LORD, they shall inherit the earth. (Ps. 37:9)
*For since the beginning of the world men have not heard . . . nor
has the eye seen any God besides you, who acts for the one who
waits for Him! (Isa. 64:4)*

I think it is important to learn the art of waiting because it requires qualities the Lord wants to encourage in us, like patience, which I need so badly. But there is another reason too. Waiting works. It is a joining of a man and God to achieve an end.

A FATHER OF LOVE

Neither death nor life . . . nor things
present nor things to come . . . shall be able to
separate us from the love of God.

ROMANS 8:38–39

One day I asked my parents, "How can I love God, someone I'm afraid of?"

"Because He loves you," came Dad's reply. "Remember that Bible verse on your Sunday school folder just last week, 'We love Him because He first loved us.' He loved you before you even knew He was there."

"But I can't feel it, or hear any words, or see a face full of love like I see your face, Dad."

"That's exactly why Jesus came down to earth, to tell us and show us that the Father in heaven is all love, is made of love. Jesus liked to say that even the best human father couldn't be half as loving or kind or generous as the heavenly Father."

GOD IS SUFFICIENT

With God all things are possible.

MATTHEW 19:26

In my own experience, I have found that God leaps to help us with anything creative. He is the Creator and when we are creating from an idea on our mind, transferring it to paper, He really does leap to help. With every single one of my books and articles, I have gotten the greatest help from God at the point where I felt most helpless myself and knew that I simply could not achieve what I had set out to do. This sounds a long way from "the power of positive thinking." I don't want to undercut Norman Vincent Peale, but perhaps there really isn't any conflict here after all. I think we're just saying the same thing in different ways. What I'm saying is that when I come to the point where I know that I'm not sufficient for any task and tell God so, then I know that He is sufficient. He's where my power of positive thinking is. And that's where the power begins to flow.

BREAD-AND-POTATO BASICS

*The LORD gives wisdom; from His
mouth come knowledge and understanding.*

PROVERBS 2:6

Writing *Christy* dragged along for so many years that I had at least four major crises with this book when I sharply questioned myself: What made me think I could write a novel? Should I struggle on with *it* or just drop it?

Each time I went back to God and tried to pray this thing through, I would be sent back to the task again.

The last time this happened I sent up prayers for the umpteenth time. And the answer I seemed to get was sort of a half-weary, half-humorous response, "Yes, you are supposed to finish this novel *because you have begun it.*" It was so emphatic that I said, "Well, Lord, I buy that one hundred percent. You're right. I would never be satisfied or happy with myself, if I didn't complete something into which I had put so much time. I'm so grateful to You for not promising me great results or anything, but just putting it on this bread-and-potato basis. I'll go and finish it."

ADVENTURES AWAIT

In all your ways acknowledge Him,
and He shall direct your paths.

PROVERBS 3:6

The other day the rent was suddenly raised sharply on some office space we are renting. It was the second raise in less than a year. I started to rail out against it, then stopped.

"What are You telling me through this, Lord?" I asked. "Are You suggesting new priorities for us? A simplification of lifestyle? Whatever it is, let me hear and receive it."

A loving God often allows mishaps to happen to us in order to get our attention. In His loving supervision of our lives, He sometimes needs to call a halt to our self-centered living. If we will then stop our rebellious railing against this interruption and instead ask a loving God what He wants to teach us, surprising revelations, giant steps forward and incalculable adventures await us.

PATIENCE TO TRUST AND WAIT

God is greater than our heart,
and knows all things.

1 JOHN 3:20

Is there in your life a cherished heart's desire taken to God over and over again in prayer, yet still unfulfilled? If so, link hands with the rest of us, and with all prayer-warriors across the centuries! No wonder Jesus had so much to say about persistence in prayer, along with His clear teaching that sometimes we will have to wait for God to move.

It's the waiting that can be so hard. Where can we find the needed patience? I think in the end, it all comes down to trust. We have to trust the Lord even when we wonder why He delays.

THE POWER OF JOY

The joy of the LORD is your strength.

NEHEMIAH 8:10

Perhaps one of the reasons many of us do not understand the power of joy is that we have been wrong in thinking of Jesus Christ as primarily "a man of sorrows, and acquainted with grief." No man with an attitude of gloom could ever have drawn little children to Him. Only a virile man who went out to meet life with unflagging zest could have attracted rugged fisherman as His disciples. Sadness couldn't last long when a man delightedly threw away his crutches or a leper went off leaping and singing on his way to show his clean new flesh to the priest.

Certainly He knew about life's problems and disappointments. . . . *In the world you will have tribulation,* He promised His disciples. *But,* He added, *be of good cheer; I have overcome the world* (John 16:33).

LOVE AND JOY

The fruit of the Spirit is love, joy, peace, longsuffering,
kindness, goodness, faithfulness, gentleness, self-control.

GALATIANS 5:22–23

Long before Jesus' day, many of the ancient Israelites had stumbled on the truth that God's love is closely akin to joy. *A merry heart does good like a medicine . . .* (Prov. 17:22). *Serve the LORD with gladness; come before His presence with singing* (Ps. 100:2).

One of Webster's definitions of joy is that of an emotion excited by the "expectation of good." The truth is that love and joy are inseparably connected. On the negative side, when we judge or are hypercritical, when we belittle or carp, love is nowhere in sight. On the positive side, love—to be love—must have joy in it; must have goodwill; must want the best for the beloved; must want to withhold no blessing—does not even ask whether the blessings are deserved.

EXPECTANT FAITH

Casting all your care upon Him, for He cares for you.

1 PETER 5:7

I tend to have a low boiling point. The dishwasher burns out, and I rail at the fact that our warranty on it expired two months before. When we trade in the tired family sedan for a gasoline-saving car, only to find it overheating within the first two weeks, I blow up at the deteriorating state of American manufacturing.

The fact that the cost of repairing both the dishwasher and the new car turns out to be minor does not bring back the peace of mind I lost.

Why am I like this? Where is my expectant faith based on God's promise that *all* things work together for good to them that love Him? (Rom. 8:28) Over and over again, personal experience has taught me that God can bring good out of every mishap, large or small. When things seem to go wrong, therefore, instead of getting so upset, why don't I try to listen harder for whatever it is that God is trying to tell me?

HEALING FROM SORROW

Surely He has borne our griefs and carried our sorrows.

ISAIAH 53:4

*H*ere are some suggestions that many of us have found helpful in the wake of sorrow:

1. By an act of will, open your heart, your arms and the door of your home to the love of God pouring to you through friends. Isolating yourself will compound your grief and delay healing.

2. Since grief is a real wound in the human spirit, know that our resurrected Lord is still the greatest Physician to the human spirit. Therefore, unabashedly pour out to Him all your questions, your fears—even your anger. Don't be afraid of offending Him by rough words; what He wants from us is complete honesty.

3. Do not allow yourself to go the "What if?" route, a temptation to every bereaved person. . . . The "What if?" route is a dead end that only heaps on remorse.

4. Read and saturate yourself in the comfort and wisdom from God's Word.

OVERCOME EVIL WITH GOOD

Repay no one evil for evil . . . but overcome evil with good.

ROMANS 12:17–21

A woman had been wronged by her husband. Filled with bitterness and the desire to hurt him, her health began to fail. Day by day her problems multiplied. Finally, she went to a friend for advice.

"Evil is a downward spiral," the friend explained. "If you return evil for evil, you'll forsake God and get on that dreadful downward spiral along with your husband. By handling this God's way, there's power here to solve all your problems. Let go of your resentments. Ask God to heal the deep hurt, and to give you a chance to return good for evil."

"Revenge hasn't worked," the woman admitted. "I'll try God's way."

Later the chance to return good came to her. With Christ's help, she managed to exhibit love and kindness. Her bitterness left; her health returned. Today she is a living testimony of the power of returning good for evil.

LOOK UP AND LIVE!

Having been justified by faith, we have
peace with God through our Lord Jesus Christ.

ROMANS 5:1

esus said, over and over, that He had not come into the world to condemn us, but to save us (John 8:15; 12:47). Apparently, He thought that any time spent in condemnation, in wallowing in our old sins and regrets, in recriminations, in kicking ourselves around the block, is wasted time. Jesus Himself spent no time berating the sinners who came to Him. His attitude was "let's get on with the positive, the creative. Let's look up and live!"

There was little old Zaccheus. He had spent his whole life on his own particular wizened brand of sin. But one day he met Jesus. It was Zaccheus' last chance to meet the Nazarene, for Jesus was even then on His way to the cross. But one meeting was enough. Jesus said, "This day, this very day, has salvation come to thy house."

FULL MEASURE, OVERFLOWING

O Lord, how manifold are Your works!
In wisdom You have made them all.

PSALM 104:24

*J*esus expected even nature to follow the laws of productivity in His Father's world. He actually cursed the fig tree that was not being productive (Matt. 21:19). The fig tree didn't even have any right to take up space in His Father's world, and not produce. The withering of the fig tree at Jesus' command was followed by some of the strongest words on faith He ever spoke (Matt. 21:21–22). Faith in whom? In God. Faith in what? In the fact that His Father, and the full weight of God's power, are on the side of productivity, creativity.

Jesus multiplied and added. He never subtracted. He multiplied the loaves and the fish, multiplied them lavishly, so that there were twelve baskets left over. Thus He showed us that the law of supply with regard to material things is at our disposal. God provided full measure, pressed down, overflowing. So I personally have found it to be.

SAFE AND LOVED

Every house is built by someone,
but He who built all things is God.

HEBREWS 3:4

Unless each of us can find answers that satisfy, we cannot trust the Creator with our dearest hopes, and so we shall have no basis for faith in God.

All of us have had contradictory experiences of the nature of God. I know I have. They run like threads through my childhood. In the very beginning, the love of my father and mother taught me of the fatherliness of God lying at the heart of the universe. Looking back at that childhood, feelings of glorious freedom and of rushing joy rise even now to meet me. Safe and loved we were, in God's world.

HANDS JOINED WITH GOD

I am the vine, you are the branches.
He who abides in me, and I in him, bears much fruit.

JOHN 15:5

What does this verse mean practically for us? It means that whatever problems we face for ourselves or our families, for the fellowship to which we belong, or our world, that is a downward spiral, we can be certain that God is against it. It means that when we step out into faith, aligning ourselves on the side of the positive, creativity of the Kingdom of God, we will find solid ground underneath our feet. For when we join hands with God, set against the powers of evil and darkness, evil does not have a chance.

It means that the next task for each one of us is to ferret out and speedily get rid of every negative attitude and thought in us. It means that with God in *any* creative uplifting enterprise, the sky is the limit. Whether it's George Müeller seeking to raise a million dollars for his orphans . . . or any of us praying for those whose needs are dear to our hearts. It means that the gates of hell shall not prevail against us.

A Bright, Shining Light

I have come as a light into the world,
that whoever believes in Me should not abide in darkness.

JOHN 12:46

Everywhere Jesus went, there was a little lighted area of the Kingdom of God on earth. Yet, He told His apostles that it was "better, . . . that He go away." Why? Because while in the flesh Jesus was subject to geographic limitations. The Kingdom of God couldn't come to the whole world that way.

"I have a plan," He told those eleven men that night, before He went out to keep His tragic rendezvous in the Garden of Gethsemane. "You will find men and women who will also say 'Yes' and 'Amen' to God. I'll send the Holy Spirit to them. Through Him each one of those people will become a light—not a light hidden under a bushel, but one shining for all the world to see deeds wrought in God. The lights will multiply. Soon the whole world will be lighted. These people will do greater works than I did. They'll say 'Yes' to God, and sin, disease, bondage, poverty, and injustice will flee away."

GOD'S KINGDOM IS CONSTRUCTIVE

God is not the author of confusion but of peace.

1 CORINTHIANS 14:33

We are told in First John, "For this purpose was the Son of God made manifest to destroy the works of the devil." And Jesus verified this by word and deed. Everything had been created by His Father—nature in all its aspects, nature which He loved and which fed and refreshed His spirit; the human mind, the human spirit, even the bodies of men. Anything destructive of any part of His Father's handiwork was the work of the devil and was not to be tolerated an instant longer than necessary.

The Kingdom is always constructive.

GOD'S PROMISES

Blessed is the man who trusts in the LORD,
and whose hope is the LORD.

JEREMIAH 17:7

I have found that God always stands behind the Bible's great promises solidly, unwaveringly, as surely as the sun rises and the tides ebb and flow.

When I need guidance—In all your ways acknowledge Him, and He shall direct your paths (Prov. 3:6).

When I have sinned and need forgiveness—If we confess our sins, He is faithful and just to forgive us our sins, and to cleanse us from all unrighteousness (1 John 1:9).

When I'm lonely and long to feel Christ's presence—Behold, I stand at the door, and knock. If anyone hears My voice and opens the door, I will come in to him and dine with him, and he with Me (Rev. 3:20).

When I am concerned by the evil in the world—You must not let yourself be distressed—you must hold on to your faith in God and to your faith in Me (John 14:1, PHILLIPS).

THE PRAYER OF HELPLESSNESS

The LORD's hand is not shortened,
that it cannot save; nor His ear heavy that it cannot hear.

ISAIAH 59:1

Why is prayer so startlingly effective when we admit our helplessness? First, because God insists upon our facing up to the true fact of our human situation. . . . This recognition . . . of our helplessness . . . deals a mortal blow to the most serious sin of all—a human independence that ignores God.

Second, we cannot learn first-hand about God—what He is like, His love for us as individuals, and His real power—so long as we are relying on ourselves and other people. . . .

So if your every human plan and calculation has miscarried; if, one by one, human props have been knocked out and doors have shut in your face, take heart. God is trying to get a message through to you: "Stop depending on inadequate human resources. Let Me handle the matter."

OBEDIENCE HONORS GOD

Let your heart therefore be loyal to the LORD our God,
to walk in His statutes and keep His commandments.

1 KINGS 8:61

Scripture clearly points out the kinds of obedience God requires of us.

To law and governmental authority—As citizens of transient, earthly kingdoms . . . we are voluntarily to subject ourselves to law and the national government over us (Titus 3:1).

To the Body of Christ on earth—"be subject one to another" (1 Pet. 5:5).

To our human family—Depending upon our individual position in the family unit, God asks of us obedience and responsibility in a chain of Divine Order, which He has established. The husband is under Christ's authority; . . . the wife is the helpmate to the husband; . . .and children are to obey their parents "in everything, for this pleases the Lord" (Col. 3:20).

GRACE FOR EVERYONE

God shows no partiality. . . . Whoever fears
Him and works righteousness is accepted by Him.

ACTS 10:34–35

Peter was given a vision of a huge sheet let down from heaven filled with all sorts of creatures, including some the Jews regarded as unclean. The meaning? Peter was to disregard the Jewish taboo on certain foods. This led into the larger truth that Gentiles who wanted to ally themselves with the infant Christian church did not have to become Jews first. That, in turn, burst into a truth so big it embraced the whole world: God was asking Peter and all of us to love everything He had made, all His older creatures and one another. Nothing—no one—is to be refused the grace and love of God.

"Aught" Against "Any"

Be kind to one another, tenderhearted,
forgiving one another, just as God in Christ forgave you.

EPHESIANS 4:32

There are no more judgmental people in the world than Christians. . . . It was certainly so in my life!

My friend David made this observations. "Well, in my life I've found that forgiving others is key to getting prayers answered. A couple of years ago I was going through one of those prayers-not-getting-beyond-the-ceiling periods and I prayed, 'Lord, I don't have enough faith. Give me the gift of faith.'

"'It isn't your faith', the reply came. 'I can see faith even if it's as small as a mustard seed. No, it's something else. . . . 'When you stand praying—forgive if ye have aught against any' (Mark 11:25). That's your trouble. That's why your prayers aren't answered. You go about with a lot of *aughts* against a lot of *anys.*'"

HAND IN HAND WITH PRAISE

Those who sow in tears shall reap in joy.

PSALM 126:5

An arresting biblical concept is that true praise and thanksgiving actually bless and magnify God; that what we do and our attitudes are important to Him for His sake, not just for ours.

The Hebrew root for *thank* also means "to acknowledge," "to confess." It is also related to the word for "hand," probably meaning the gestures used in worship.

Thus confession of wrong goes hand in hand with praise because it is the other side of God's sovereignty.

Anything but praise attributes more power to someone or something than to God.

CHOOSE BLESSINGS

How great is Your goodness,
which You have laid up for those who fear You.

PSALM 31:19

Before formally commissioning Joshua as his successor, Moses gave a farewell charge to Israel. This charge is the book of Deuteronomy.

Reading this book is like looking through a window into the amplitude of Moses' spirit. In his speech there is no note of an old man's sentimental nostalgia, rather the entire thrust is into the future. Warm with feeling and persuasively eloquent, Moses focused on this one significant point: "I have set before you life and death, blessing and cursing; therefore choose life" (Deut. 30:19).

The rest of the Old Testament narrative tells us what happened. All too often the descendants of those to whom Moses had given his charge did not "choose life." History records that these descendants did go into captivity literally as well as spiritually.

Each generation then, as now, has a choice: life or death . . . the blessing or the curse.

OBEDIENCE WITHOUT RESERVATION

Whoever hears these sayings of Mine, and does them,
I will liken him to a wise man who built his house on the rock.

MATTHEW 7:24

How often Jesus told us we would be wise men and women to obey His instructions. He even went on to say that when we go through great difficulty—such as torrential rain and floods and storm winds beating against our house—it will not collapse and we won't be in real danger if we obey Him (Matt. 7:25).

Yet, unlike earthly kings, God does not want our obedience out of fear. Our obedience to Him is the fruit of lives growing in the rich soil of love and trust. Our obedience is to be at once both the result of our loving God and also the proof of our love (John 14:21–23). As with human love, we are going to be capable of loving only to the extent that we abandon ourselves to another with no reservations.

ABUNDANT LIFE

Though now you do not see Him, yet believing,
you rejoice with joy inexpressible and full of glory.

1 PETER 1:8

God's promises to His children as recorded in the Bible are our legacy. But in order to obtain this inheritance, an heir has to step up and claim it. Here is one of those greatest of all promises for you to claim for yourself and your children: "And we know that all things work together for good to them that love God, to them who are the called according to His purpose" (Rom. 8:28).

I've never known this promise to fail. Over and over God achieves this miracle of bringing something beautiful and good and positive out of life's wreckage. . . .

Jesus said that He came into our world for the specific purpose of giving us life, more abundant life. He is not the God of the tomb, but of resurrection morning. Give your life and your problems over to Him. I can guarantee that He has an answer tailor-made for *your* needs by One who loves you personally and wants to see you laugh again.

GET ON WITH LIFE

The LORD will give grace and glory;
no good thing will He withhold from
those who walk uprightly.

PSALM 84:11

A divine impatience on the part of Jesus, made Him unwilling to tolerate for an instant longer than was necessary, any negative, degrading quality in human life. Zaccheus had been a lifetime in sin. Jesus said, "*This day* has salvation come to thy house."

There was a man blind from birth. When he met the Master he was a grown man. Jesus cured Him, though the man did not even know who Jesus was.

The man at the pool at Bethsaida had been a cripple, unable to stand for thirty-eight years. Jesus asked him, "Do you *really* want to be made well? All right then, pick up your bed and walk. Get on with your life. You've wasted enough time." And the man did get on with life.

SUBMISSION TO GOD'S WILL

He is Lord of lords, and King of kings. . . .

REVELATION 17:14

It was agony, such agony that as Jesus knelt there in the garden He could not have been aware of the beauty all around Him. The valley under the brow of the hill was washed in moonlight. Below Him the brook Kedron rippled and sang over stones and through rushes. Around Him were the myrtle trees, palms, and fig trees that melted into the olive groves. And in the enclosed Garden of Gethsemane, all around His prostrate figure were the leaves and trunks of the olive trees silvered by filtering moonlight. . . . This was not a world that Christ, the man, wanted to leave.

Was there a moment when He wondered *how* to pray about the terrible alternatives before Him? If so, in the end He knew that only one prayer could release the power that was needed to lift a sin-ridden world: "Dear Father, . . . it is not what I want, but what You want."

GOD HAS NO GRANDCHILDREN

I call to remembrance the genuine faith that is
in you, which dwelt first in your grandmother . . .
and your mother. . . .

2 TIMOTHY 1:5

am convinced that God never meant for anything about the Christian life to be vague, least of all the steps by which we enter into a meaningful relationship with Him. The obscurity must surely be on our side, not God's.

Growing up in a believing family is not to be undervalued. It is still the ideal beginning, because it is the foundation of the happiest possible childhood. Yet I know now that something more is needed; each human being must enter into Life with Christ for himself. There is no such thing as inheriting Christianity.

December

God has designed us for happiness.

He has created us for peace and joy.

GIVE LOVE AWAY

To whom much is given . . . much will be required.

LUKE 12:48

Mother's bank account was her faith in the Lord, her absolute trust that the promise of "give and it shall be given unto you" was a certainty. The wellspring of Mother's supreme confidence was the knowledge that God would provide out of His limitless supply. "And the more you give," we heard her say so often, "the more you receive. God simply will not let us out-give Him."

Out of this solid wealth, this certainty, Mother could always afford to give to others, not just material things, but a spark of imagination, a glimmer of hope, a thrust of courage—things that often helped others to produce the needed material things.

As Christmas comes this year why don't we all try giving out of what we think is our scarcity. . . . Let's be creative, let's be loving, and above all, let us not worry about our capacity to give. As my Mother would say, you never have so little that you can't give some of it away!

THE WELL-TRAVELED ROAD

And the LORD went before them . . . to lead the way.

EXODUS 13:21

od deals differently with each of us. He knows no "typical" case. He seeks us out at a point in our own need and longing and runs down the road to meet us. This individualized treatment should delight rather than confuse us, because it so clearly reveals the highly personal quality of God's love and concern.

The way to God is a clearly marked, well-traveled road. Only one question remains to us: Do we really want to find our way down that road?

God challenges us to place our faith in Him rather than in fallible human beings: "Taste and see that the Lord is good." In my experience this is not an ivory-tower approach. It is the only effectual one. Try accepting God's help in the small details of your daily life—and you, too, will experience His loving care.

GOD'S IN CONTROL

With men this is impossible,
but with God all things are possible.

MATTHEW 19:26

Not a single spiritual quality—faith, peace of mind, joy, patience, the ability to love the wretched and the unlovely—can we work up by self-effort. Anyone who has tried, knows that she cannot.

In helplessness alone there would be no value; our situation would be intolerable if Jesus had left us there. But He went on to add, "With God all things are possible."

"All things!" This is as audacious a statement as the opposite was, "Apart from me, ye can do nothing." Jesus must be saying that there is nothing in Heaven or in earth over which God does not have control.

PRAYER BEHIND CLOSED DOORS

In the night His song shall be with me—
a prayer to the God of my life.

PSALM 42:8

George Müeller set aside one hour each day for prayer. As punctually as a Swiss watch, George would retire to his room at the allotted time. On his knees he could concentrate on meeting his Lord, pouring out to God his wishes and hopes and dreams for his work and the needs of his orphans. Once every week, he met with all his associates in a session of prayer—also behind closed doors.

There was something so irresistibly challenging about Müeller's formula that despite his aversion to publicity, the news traveled and purses were eagerly opened. Starting with one rented house, two workers, and forty-three children, in time there were five new buildings and 110 workers for 2,050 orphans. In all, during his lifetime, 121,000 orphans were sheltered, fed, educated—a million and a half pound sterling administered. The work is still going on as a monument to faith, and at its heart was prayer in secret.

GIVE YOUR DREAMS TO GOD

God is faithful, by whom you were called
into the fellowship of His Son, Jesus Christ our Lord.

1 CORINTHIANS 1:9

Hand your dream over to God, and leave it in His keeping. There seem to be periods when the dream is like a seed that must be planted in the dark earth and left there to germinate. There is not a time of passiveness on our part. There are things we can and must do—fertilizing, watering, weeding—hard work and self-discipline.

But the growth of that seed, the mysterious and irresistible burgeoning of life in dark and in secret, that is God's part of the process. We must not keep digging up our dream, examining and measuring it to see how it is coming along. . . . Along with the dream, He gives us whatever graces, patience, and stamina it takes to see the dream through to fruition.

ASKING THE FATHER FOR HELP

I am a companion of all who fear You,
and of those who keep Your precepts.

PSALM 119:63

Prayer, at its humble and most basic, is *asking*. The prayer of a child quite simply running to its father for help. This is what we would rediscover in an age of perplexity—how do we run to the Father?

In this day, the halls and classrooms of the School of Prayer are crowded as never before because our needs press upon us with new urgency: worldwide economic crises, marriage problems on the rise, . . . drug addiction, . . . alcoholism. . . . No wonder we rush to school! Our thirst is deep, our eagerness to learn is enormous.

What good news it is that our very inadequacy is the master key swinging wide the door to His adequacy. Who but Jesus could ever have thought of a plan like that!

A SPARK OF THE DIVINE

A man can receive nothing
unless it has been given him from heaven.

JOHN 3:27

*G*enesis tells us that the Creator-God worked for five days fashioning perfectly every detail of planet earth and its surrounding cosmos. On the sixth day He created the first man, Adam. Only afterwards, on the seventh day, did God rest.

But the man Adam (representative of all of us humans) began his life with Sabbath-rest because the work had been completed. The man's only task was to receive God's bounty from His hands—the beauty and fragrance and goodness of the flowers and the fruit; the beasts and the birds.

There's a note of courtliness in the ancient account as we see the creatures, large and small, being brought to Adam for him to name. The man was God's own steward of the Eden-paradise. . . . It's the first hint in Scripture of the respect God always has for every human being.

THE CIRCLE OF PRAYER

For as many as are led by the
Spirit of God, these are sons of God.

ROMANS 8:14

believe the Claiming Prayer to be the crown of all ways of prayer because it inscribes a completed circle between earth and heaven, thus meeting the conditions of prayer power. For the purpose of all prayer is to find God's will and to make that will our prayer. . . .

Thus we go to God with a problem, seeking light on it. We give God a chance to speak to us either through Scripture or through His quiet voice in our hearts. This part makes half of the circle as our need sweeps up to God.

Then God points out to us one of His promises that applies to our situation. Our claiming of this promise will complete the circle—from heaven to earth.

This promise is the handle of faith that we can grasp in prayer.

SPIRITUAL "VITAMINS"

These words which I command you, . . .
you shall teach . . . diligently to your children.

DEUTERONOMY 6:6–7

ast week I produced a "Vitamin Box" of dozens of favorite passages for my family. I used a concordance and looked up words such as *strength, food, bread, water, hunger,* and *thirst.* Other cards were culled from Christ's own words. Now before blessing the food at each meal, we pass the box, and one of the children chooses a card to read aloud. The nourishment is most effective when the life-giving words of Scripture are memorized and so become the permanent possessions of mind and heart.

SELF-PITY IS SIN

This is the confidence that we have in Him,
that if we ask anything according to His will, He hears us.

1 JOHN 5:14

*S*ince self-pity is a sin, then clearly it has be to dealt with as a sin. A sin because since I belong to Jesus; it is He who has control over my life. Thus He overrules everything that He "allows" to happen to me—overrules it for *good*.

My part is to trust Him as a loving Heavenly Father in each of these adverse circumstances. I am to watch expectantly for the "good". . . the new adventure He has for me . . . the open door I am to go through toward the better way to which He is leading me.

So, given all that, what is there to have self-pity about? . . . Each time I am tempted toward despairing self-pity, I must rebuke it, reject it, and turn immediately to praise.

ADMITTING OUR NEEDS

*He who has begun a good work in you
will complete it until the day of Jesus Christ.*

PHILIPPIANS 1:6

*C*risis brings us face to face with our inadequacy and our inadequacy in turn leads us to the inexhaustible sufficiency of God. This is the power of helplessness, a principle written into the fabric of life.

At this point some realist will surely say, "I cannot accept this helplessness theory. It goes against everything I have been taught about rugged individualism. Where would our nation be now, if it weren't for the pioneer spirit of our forefathers who refused to admit defeat in the face of tremendous odds? America was built by men who scorned weakness and helplessness."

It is precisely here that the realist misses the point about this principle. For the realization of helplessness in no sense precludes a courageous pioneer independence. Being adventuresome does not mean that we cannot admit our need for God.

A Door of Hope

I will give back her vineyards to her,
and transform her Valley of Troubles into a Door of Hope.

HOSEA 2:15 TLB

A small child was killed by a drunken driver. Since God is love and has all power, why did that happen? I cannot believe that such a tragedy was in God's original perfect plan for that child. Human willfulness and disobedience have, since the Garden of Eden, temporarily upset God's perfect plans.

But I do believe that evil must have God's permission in order to touch our lives (Job 1:1-12), and that by the time any event reaches us, God already has a plan by which He can bring good out of the difficulty.

God is the only One who can make the valley of trouble a door of hope. He always wants to use trouble as the starting-point for real creativity. This miracle requires only our unshakable faith in the goodness of God, and our thoughtful cooperation. In the end, no evil can defeat the Lord of our lives.

CREATIVE THROUGH CHRIST

Pursue righteousness, godliness,
faith, love, patience, gentleness.

1 TIMOTHY 6:11

When achievement has come because of our helplessness linked to God's power, it has a rightness about it that no amount of self-inspired striving can have. Furthermore, when achievement comes this way, it does not bear in it the seeds of increasing egocentricity that success sometimes brings. Because we know that ideas and the ability to implement them flowed into us from somewhere beyond our selves, we can be objective about our good fortune. We know, too, that if, in the future, the connection with the Source of creativity is broken, there will not be success the next time. . . .

God has never allowed me the fulfillment of a soul's sincere desire without first putting me through an acute realization of my inadequacy and my need for help.

MORE BLESSED TO GIVE

It is more blessed to give than to receive.

ACTS 20:35

The year I was eleven I learned for myself that it actually is more blessed to give than to receive.

I started my Christmas preparations quite early in September. As the gifts were completed, I piled them up on two closet shelves cleared for that purpose. There were small rustic Yule logs with fat red candles, meant for mantel and table decorations; . . . pillowcases I had embroidered; tea towels I had hemmed; crepe-paper dolls with bouffant skirts supposed to hide powder boxes on dressing tables. It was the only year I did it.

How much my relatives appreciated these gifts I do not know. But the effort provided me with an inner satisfaction that I've never forgotten. The proof is that this one Christmas stands out glowingly above every other Christmas of my growing-up years.

START LIVING AGAIN

We walk by faith, not by sight.

2 CORINTHIANS 5:7

We are told that we must walk by faith, but *how* do we get faith? We know that when we turn some matter over to the Lord, worrying about it is a sure sign of lack of trust. Yet worry buzzes like a fly at our consciousness. We must not harbor resentments; but we find the resentments sticking like molasses. We know that grieving for those who are rejoicing in the Lord's presence dishonors Christ and them. But we can't turn off grief like a faucet. So how can we start living again?

The greatest single secret that I've learned is applicable to these situations as well as to many others. The secret is that our emotions are not the real *us*. The governing power inside us—the spring of all our actions—is the will. Before God we are responsible only for the set of that will, whether it is still under the control of self or whether we have handed our free will back to the God who gave it. Our Maker knows perfectly well that our emotions are unruly, and that He alone can handle them.

HANG ONTO GOD'S LOVE

Commit your way to the LORD,
trust also in Him, and He shall bring it to pass.

PSALM 37:5

any Scriptures emphasize our need to have faith in God. The above verse takes us a step further. It not only admonishes us to trust, it promises that when we do, God will act in a supernatural way to answer our need. Dwell on that for a moment. We trust, God acts. A mind-blowing premise.

Yet total, all-out trust on our part is not as easy as it first seems. There are periods when God's face is shrouded, when His dealings with us will *appear* as if He does not care, when He seems not to be acting like a true Father. Can we then hang onto the fact of His love and His faithfulness and that He *is* a prayer-answering God? "Roll" the entire burden onto His shoulders, as He bade us do, step out and *take the first step* with bare, no-evidence-at-all faith.

And lo, He does take over gloriously, doing what we literally cannot do for ourselves.

THE GIFT OF TIME

If you know how to give good gifts to your children . . .
how much more will your Father who is in heaven
give good things to those who ask Him!

MATTHEW 7:11

The most cherished gift we parents can give our children during the Yuletide season is our time—ourselves. No gift, no matter how expensive, can take the place of this.

What are some of the gifts time can bestow on our children? Help them make the gifts they give away; . . .

cut the family Christmas tree

create a Christmas tree for the birds in the backyard

organize a cookie-making evening; . . .

plan a little family service to be held in the living room on Christmas morning.

It takes time, much time—but our children will never forget a bit of it. Out of it will come deep and lasting satisfactions—the discovery of the joy of giving and a feeling of closeness to family and community.

JESUS' JOY

My soul magnifies the Lord,
and my spirit has rejoiced in God my Savior.

LUKE 1:46–47

The real source of Jesus' joy is given us in unforgettable words first spoken by the Psalmist and centuries later by the author of Hebrews: "You have loved righteousness and hated lawlessness; therefore God, Your God, has anointed You with the oil of gladness more than Your companions" (Heb. 1:9).

He who knew no sin and *is* righteousness, had a personality sparkling and overflowing with a degree of gladness that none of us can match. How could it be otherwise! . . .

Jesus is the *only* righteous One, therefore the only finally joyous One. But this joy He longs to share with all who will receive it.

KINGDOM OF RELATIONSHIPS

*Walk in love, as Christ also has
loved us and given Himself for us.*

EPHESIANS 5:2

am amazed to see, how frequently the giving
of gifts is mentioned in the Bible. And how in
every case the gift springs out of and is symbolic of a
relationship, good or bad. Rebekah accepts gifts of jewelry and
clothing, symbolic of her acceptance if Isaac as her husband.
Jacob tries to give a lavish present of livestock to the brother he
has wronged, but Esau refuses. Later on, Jacob singles out one of
his sons for the gift of a beautiful coat, demonstrating his
favoritism and fostering jealousy among the brothers. Wise
Men bring gifts to an Infant—gold, which acknowledges their
King, frankincense their God, myrrh their Redeemer.

It should not surprise us that the person-to-person dimension
is important. The Kingdom of God is the kingdom of right relationships. That's what matters to Him.

When the relationship is right, how precious the gift becomes.

CHRISTMAS WITH LOVE

Grant us that we ... might serve Him ...
in holiness and righteousness ... all the days of our life.

LUKE 1:74–75

When Christmas ceases to be pure delight and becomes a burden, at that point we have lost Christmas. All too often, we adults buy presents with money we do not have. We wrap gifts with time we begrudge. We give them to acquaintances we do not cherish. There is a lesson here: what we do not do with love and relaxation is wasted effort.

For the over-privileged, this insistence on putting ourselves into our gifts takes self-control. For the underprivileged, it takes faith and God-given creativity. All three are qualities worth cultivating.

PEACE ON EARTH

Be at peace among yourselves.

1 THESSALONIANS 5:13

oday our civilization cries out for forgiveness. Husbands and wives need it . . . Parents and children . . . Friends . . . Statesmen. Businessmen and labor leaders need it.

Yes, and nations. Jesus would tell us that we Americans must forgive the Japanese for Pearl Harbor, just as the Japanese must forgive us for Hiroshima. The Jews have so much for which to forgive the Germans. And the Germans have much to forgive the Russians; and the Russians the Germans. Have the Ethiopians forgiven the Italians? And what about the Israelis and the Arabs with so much bitterness on both sides. If the wounds of millions are to be healed, what other way is there except through forgiveness?

Jesus, at least, gives us no alternative. The command is stern. The terms are set. "But if you do not forgive men their trespasses, neither will your Father forgive your trespasses" (Matt. 6:15).

God's forgiveness and man's are one.

FAMILY TRADITIONS

Always pursue what is good both for yourselves and for all.

1 THESSALONIANS 5:15

From the cradle to the end of life, each of us feels isolated inside the lonely shell of self. Built into us is the need to make contact with other human beings, so the act of doing things together in a family reaches deep inside a child and satisfies his thirst for community, for fellowship, for proof that he isn't alone in the world.

That's why traditions based on family activities give the individual security and strengthen family ties. The traditions return again and again to remind us of the imperishables that help make up the foundation of our lives—love of family, companionship, humor, enthusiasm, gratitude. Our life would not be worth living without these qualities. But every parent knows the difficulty of teaching them to our children, who are born self-centered. They can't *see* humor, or handle love, or touch gratitude. Yet love is every bit as real as granite, and gratitude is just as much a reality as fire, so these verities must be dramatized for our children . . . through the medium of family traditions.

ONE HEART AND SOUL

*Let us consider one another in order
to stir up love and good works, not forsaking the
assembling of ourselves together.*

HEBREWS 10:24–25

Christianity was never meant to be a lone-sheep experience. One reason the first Christians received so much helpful guidance was that they had the *koinonia*, a corporate fellowship that made them "of one heart and soul." It was in this setting that illumination, inspiration, and guidance flourished.

Every one of us needs as much of the *koinonia* as we can find. We must seek out mature Christian friends with whom we can share questions, problems, and the joys of discovery. Ideas will often come to our corporate mind that would not come to us in isolation. And sometimes God does speak directly through these friends. At the very least, their love, perspective, and common sense will help to steer us clear of wild tangents.

GIFTS ARE SECONDARY

You yourselves are taught by God to love one another.

1 THESSALONIANS 4:9

hristmas—the time for giving and receiving gifts—is here again. Nowadays the store decorations go up before Thanksgiving is over. Pondering the commercialism that seems to characterize this holiday season, I began to wonder if the Bible had anything to say about gifts and giving that might be helpful.

When I turned to it, one portion of the Sermon on the Mount seemed especially pertinent. If we stand in the temple, Jesus said, about to offer a gift to God, and suddenly remember that a friend has a grudge or resentment against us, we are to postpone giving the gift. We are to go and be reconciled to our friend, then come back and offer our gift to God; only then will He receive our offerings and bless us. Relationships are primary, He seems to be saying; gifts secondary.

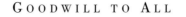

GOODWILL TO ALL

Glory to God in the highest,
and on earth peace, goodwill toward men.

LUKE 2:14

The feeling of closeness to other people, of the togetherness of all human beings, flourishes at Christmastime. During this one brief season each year our frustrated old world almost achieves the Kingdom of God on earth. For the term "Kingdom of God" really means "kingdom of right relationships," and this is specifically what the Christ child came to earth to make possible.

The spirit that finds it all but impossible to hold a grudge, a spirit of friendliness, and love born out of sheer goodwill—this is the Kingdom of God on earth. Even during the Yuletide season, grownups step into that kingdom a little warily, somewhat self-consciously. . . . In doing so, they prove to the most cynical of us that the Kingdom of heaven on earth—the "goodwill toward men" of which the Christmas angels sang—is no fantasy.

GOD'S TIMING

It is not for you to know the times or seasons
which the Father has put in His own authority.

ACTS 1:7

Jesus had a great deal to say about His Father's timing, the principle that there is a God-given sequence and rate of growth for everything in His Creation: " . . . first the blade, then the head, after that the full grain in the head" (Mark 4:28).

"The time is fulfilled, and the kingdom of God is at hand," (Mark 1:15) Jesus might say. Or when certain disciples were trying to get Him to act prematurely, "My time is not yet come . . ." (John 7:6). The emphasis was always *His* timing.

God does have his "fullness of time" for the answer to each prayer. It follows then that He alone knows the magnitude of the changes that have to be wrought in us before we can receive our hearts' desires. He alone knows the changes and interplay of external events that must take place before our prayer can be answered.

GOING WHERE GOD LEADS

He who calls you is faithful, who also will do it.

1 THESSALONIANS 5:24

The New Testament attaches no time tags to its promises of guidance. When I first became interested in this subject, I could not ignore Peter Marshall's oft-reiterated conviction that God can and does communicate His will to modern men and women just as He did to those in biblical times. In his life, Peter did not often have the guidance of the inner Voice. More frequently his direction came through providential circumstances plus a strong inner feeling of rightness about a particular decision. He was thus led from Scotland to the United States to enter the ministry when he thought he wanted to go to China. When the door to China shut in his face, he tried for home-mission work in Scotland. That door closed too. Through a series of remarkable circumstances, the way to the United States then opened. Certainly this was God's guidance to an extraordinarily fruitful life.

PATIENT PRAYERS

The LORD is good to those who wait for Him,
to the soul who seeks Him.

LAMENTATIONS 3:25

Part of our problem in praying for our children, is the time lag, the necessary slow maturation of our prayers. But that's the way of God's rhythm in nature. For instance, the hen must patiently sit on her eggs to incubate them before the baby chicks hatch.

With this picture in mind, Dr. Glenn Clark suggests that we parents spend some time each day for at least a week thinking through our hearts' deepest desires for our children. After listing them on paper, ask for Jesus' mind on them, sifting out everything superficial or selfish until we have reached the kernel of the Spirit's hopes and dreams for this person.

Then copy these hopes in the form of prayers onto slips of paper cut in the shape of eggs and insert them between the pages of some favorite Bible—signifying leaving them in God's keeping.

WILLING TO WAIT

Let us not grow weary while doing good,
for in due season we shall reap if we do not lose heart.

GALATIANS 6:9

The Lord seems constantly to use waiting as a tool for bringing us the very best of His gifts. He made the children of Israel wait generations for their freedom from slavery in Egypt. Because of their stubborn disobedience, they had to wait forty years before they were ready to enter the Promised Land. . . . The whole story of the Old Testament is the patient waiting for "the fullness of time" of the Savior's birth. And after Jesus' Acension those gathered in the upper room had to wait a full ten days for the coming of the Holy Spirit. . . .

Waiting seems to be a kind of acted-out prayer that is required more often and honored more often than I could understand until I saw what remarkable faith-muscles this act develops. For isn't it true that waiting demands patience, persistence, trust, expectancy—all the qualities we are continually beseeching God to give us?

BLESSED MERCY

Blessed are the merciful, for they shall obtain mercy.

MATTHEW 5:7

I have marveled sometimes at the number of far-out wayfarers who are led to my door and end up becoming my close friends. Ex-alcoholics, ex-sexaholics, ex-convicts, . . . I could go on and on. . . .

When I read the Gospels, I find that the same kind of far-out folks were Jesus' friends. In fact, over and over, He was criticized for this. But He loved them, and very simply, I do too. Those who have been sunk in the dark night of the soul before the Light found them, have something we "good" church people can never know. Jesus pinpointed what that something is when He commented, "to whom little is forgiven the same loves little" (Luke 7:47).

I have learned that no human being can sink too low for the Love and Light to rescue him, . . . and heavenly hosannas still ring out so loudly as almost to split the sky, as each lost and staying sheep is hauled back from the abyss of self-destruction.

A FRESH NEW YEAR

He who overcomes shall inherit all things,
and I will be his God and he shall be My son.

REVELATION 21:7

There is a longing in my heart for the new year to be better than the old one, with a clean, bright beginning.

I have a new perspective now. That new horizon was my brother's last legacy to me as he died without warning of heart failure last year on a sunshiny August afternoon. That brought it home so sharply: Our mortality is very real. Bob was so much younger than I.

I see it now more clearly than ever before. . . . We are but strangers passing through this life on earth. Like Bob, we, too—all of us—have another destination. Our arrival there is but a continuation of our journey here. So what we are, how we use our brief days, what we do with our mortal lives is of eternal significance.